Surfing on a Banana Peel

Warning: Spiritual Evolution Ahead!

Brona Fanelle

Surfing on a Banana Peel

Warning: Spiritual Evolution Ahead!

Brona Fanelle

Translated by Jaroslav Kalfar

Surfing on a Banana Peel

Warning: Spiritual Evolution Ahead!

Brona Fanelle

www.SurfingonaBananaPeel.com

ISBN-13 978-0-9883624-1-3

Translated by Jaroslav Kalfar

Cover design by Tereza Svarcova Bellodi

Printed in the United States of America

This book is dedicated to my parents, Jerry, Veronika,

Tereza, Joao Marko and Agata.

Thank you for your unconditional love and support.

Table Contents

"The first forty years of life give us the text; the next forty supply the commentary on it."

Arthur Schopenhauer

"I entered the next forty years, and wrote this book."

Brona Fanelle

PART ONE

Only a Fool Walks in the Dark

Introduction

When you walk along the California coast, you see many people holding surfing boards, waiting for waves to break. The right one will allow them to momentarily become masters of the ocean surface. They look for balance. Surfing is the perfect metaphor for life. It is dynamic and unpredictable, you never know how strong the wave will be and how far it will toss you. Staying on top of the board of life events is not easy – sometimes you're on the bottom, then you climb back to the top. Waves have complete control and you look for guidance, different location, weather…

I too looked for advice on how to surf through life. I can't help but smile when I think of my lifelong determination to find myself and the meaning of life, its laws and functions. During the frantic search, I committed so many personal missteps and mistakes. My desire to peek beneath the curtains of the past and future, interest in reading about spiritualism, and the refreshing novelty of the subject finally thrust me into a brand new, twenty-five years long journey.

I turned over every stone and looted the spiritual sections of libraries and bookshops on both continents I called home during that quarter-century of my life. I can say with confidence that I collected enough knowledge to call myself a spiritual scholar. I read hundreds of books and tried out dozens of spiritual techniques. The more I knew, the more clearly I could see the contradictions between teachings. I couldn't find sufficiently strong connections. As a former teacher and later a journalist, I was haunted by the inevitable, capital "WHY." I couldn't find the answer for a long time. I clearly felt that I was missing a foundation, building the second floor of a house without even planning out the first. Less is more. I had no choice but to return to the basics and find a beginning. I stopped looking for the right way in books, and decided to create it on my own. I could no longer wait in a dark corner for someone else to turn on the light. I had to find the stupid switch myself.

My mother's serious illness stopped me in my tracks. Experience from this life period taught me to accept the ocean waves and other circumstances, and I stopped looking for ways to change them. Unexpectedly, this painful time showed me the path to inner balance, and I can stand tall even while surfing on a slippery banana peel in midst of a roaring ocean storm. I'm in control of my own life, and I don't share that control with random circumstances.

I'm happy to say that I no longer encounter unexpected tragic events, and I've made significant advancements in my spiritual development. I found a simple recipe to leading my own life without anyone's help, and getting rid of dramatic situations. This recipe is not dependent on my health, age, gender, nationality, residence, social status or money. Anyone can peek beneath the hidden spiritual curtain and access previously unavailable information. Spiritual independence is worth the required personal discipline and everyday routine.

But first – let's face the hard reality that preceded these revelations.

1.Power of Hydrogen Situation

My mom got sick. Cancer was the doctor's diagnosis. My mother decided to have the surgery. After surgical removal of the tumor, she refused chemotherapy. She announced that health does not come from doctors, but nature, and started looking into natural healing alternatives. She refused pills and the usual chemotherapy.

I set aside my spiritual pilgrimage and went to fight alongside my mother. In order to give her maximum support, I was ready to accept major lifestyle choices. I searched the internet, magazines and books for any usable tips. From available sources, the two of us found out a very basic fact: if the inner human system remains acidic for a long time, sickness comes, and sick cells can only be healed by following correct nutritional guidelines. Otto Warburg, a German doctor who won the Nobel in 1931 and discovered the causes of cancer, found that cancer cells can be created during the fermentation of glucose. He also proved that cancerous cells can only live in an acidic environment. As far as I can remember, despite this hundred year old discovery, every doctor's visit I've had was followed with doses of chemically manufactured medicine that eased my pain at the cost of rise in acidity and decline of my overall health. I had read that human blood maintains a stable value on the scale of acidity between 7.35pH and 7.45pH. Any rise or fall of blood pH had to be regulated by the body to maintain a stable value, otherwise the person would die. To strike this balance, the system had to wash out calcium from bones, hair, muscle and teeth. The objective was never to create an alkaline organism, but to make sure it wasn't permanently acidic. High acidity created waste that usually settled on the most vulnerable parts of the organism. While young, the body maintained the acidity levels easily by taking the readily available neutralizing material from young bones, connective tissue, etc. As the body aged, however, the calcium levels ran out. Acid couldn't be neutralized, and so it settled in joints and cartilage, causing osteoporosis, painful infections, aging.

The body did have a mechanism to eliminate acids, but it only worked under very specific conditions. It could've been very easily interrupted by, for example, lack of water, which foiled the body's natural process of carrying the acids into kidneys and flushing them out of the body. Some cells died under this acid contamination. Dead cells produced more acids. Those that survived adapted to the new conditions, lost contact with the brain, mutated, grew and reproduced uncontrollably. The body's very last line of defense was creating a tumor, a protective coating of sorts, which would protect the carrier for a while longer and give them one last chance. By the way, the pH value of a malignant tumor is between 3.0 and 3.5, because it forms from acidic human cells and mold. Only in a body that is alkaline, not acidic, does the cancer cell have no chance of surviving.

Every cell of every living organism contains flickering particles that have been dismissed by doctors as useless junk. But the results of specialized research confirmed these particles are symbiotic somatids that control the growth of cells and their division, and disconnect dead or mutated cells. Every day, a few hundred cells make an appearance inside each one of us. The somatids are a foundation of a well-functioning immune system and therefore enemies of cancer growth. To perform their duties they need a high pH. In cases where the pH value is permanently lower than 5, meaning the organism is consistently acidic, the somatids turn into hostiles. They cease to protect us and weaken our immune system, allowing cancer cells to commence their work.

Acids have a destructive effect on metal and stone, so it goes without saying what kind of damage they can do to a human body. Through exercise and resulting practice of deep breathing, we can lower the acidity of our bodies. While young, we exercise and are generally more active, but this changes as we age – that is why the rates of cancer occurrences are higher in older people. The skin is the biggest organ in the human body, and needs regular scrubbing to help the excretion of acids through the pores.

And with healthy non-acidic foods, prepared without microwaves, chemicals, heat, or any other method that devalues it, we can get rid of cancer on our own, without any help.

I wrote out a long list of acidic and basic foods and studied them to understand their properties. Generally, it seemed that the foods we consider tastiest were the worst for our health. I focused on base-forming foods and learned that though some of them taste acidic, inside of the body they act as basic. Lemons are a good example of this. The main rule is to avoid mixing proteins and carbohydrates, thus not eating animal-based foods and plant foods at the same time.

The result of mixing plant and animal food is fermentation in the small intestine and decay in the large intestine. Poisonous toxins are created during the fermentation and decay, and these toxins cause rise in acidity of the body. Acidity of the organism is also caused by shallow breathing, lack of movement and sleep, coffee, tea, overeating, stress, anger, negative emotions, chemicals and toxins that are, unfortunately, included in cleaning products, hair dye, shampoo, lipstick, cosmetics, artificial textiles, and many other everyday conveniences.

My mother immediately proved herself to be a practical woman. She verified that the only safe multipurpose laundry detergent was Borax, a natural powder that dissolves in water. She mixed four liters of water with 1/8 cup of Borax and started using the mixture as dish soap. Dry Borax turned out to be a wonderful "green cleaning" product and a cost effective one as well. To eliminate stains, she used alcohol, vinegar and baking soda. We often visited the numerous web discussion forums to get variety of information from people willing to share their valuable experiences. A healer told me once that watermelons belong in the vegetable group, not fruits, and has strong alkaline effects. He revealed that their pH number is 9. A few days later, another reader warned us: "Do not buy watermelons at Fruitland, they do not have pH 9. A urine test strip showed my pH was only 6.5 after the consumption of eight kilograms of watermelon." The watermelon gentleman obviously did not read all of the healer's advice, otherwise he would've known that before the consumption, his organism was highly acidic and the watermelon lost part of its alkalinity while balancing things out. The alkalinity of the food and resulting alkalinity of the body after acid reduction are two different things. Some people have bodies so acidic that it takes a while before the base-forming foods assert their dominance. The human organism can very quickly alkalize apple vinegar, baking soda, watermelon and raw green cucumber.

During my detox, the poisonous materials left my body through urine. The toxins were acidic despite my strictly alkaline diet, as litmus test strips showed. After the first and biggest layer of toxins was flushed out, my pH automatically increased. The litmus test strips are very effective and easily accessible in pharmacies and health food stores, and I found the urine testers more reliable than the saliva testers. At first we monitored alkalinity in my urine frequently throughout the day; after the levels of acid fell, we scaled down to testing only few times per day. Usually, my morning pH value was around 6.5, and during my afternoon consumption of homemade fruit juices and whole fruit, my pH climbed up to 8. It was sufficient to measure the higher pH once a day, to make sure the body wasn't permanently acidic. The value of acidity and alkalinity does not need to be consistent, and alternations throughout the day are to be expected. My mother's pH values were different due to her illness, but changed with the same pattern over a longer period of time.

I still do not understand why modern medicine refuses functional, logical practices and only concerns itself with easing pain through medication and solving the consequences of illnesses. The most important thing, that is, the actual cause of illness, is swept under the rug and ignored. But if we were to combine medical science and nature, we could completely eliminate illness and regenerate the human body without any side effects. Animals living in the wild do not consume pills and therefore do not voluntarily destroy their livers and kidneys. This is because they do not know doctors.

"The only way to keep your health is to eat what you don't want, drink what you don't like, and do what you'd rather not."
-Mark Twain

We bought a juicer and drank nothing but fresh vegetable and fruit juices every afternoon, as advised by the books of Dr. Norman Walker and Mr. and Mrs. Diamond. Strongly alkalizing were fresh juices made from watermelon and cucumbers, red beets, carrots, parsley, celery, apples, and lemons. It was important to avoid vegetables and fruits that were not yet ripe, as they retain high levels of acidity.

Fruits, veggies and nuts, especially almonds, formed the basis of our menu. Almonds blended for five minutes with water make for the most delicious almond milk I've ever had.

"The first wealth is health." -Ralph Waldo Emerson

Enzymes enable us to digest food. Because they are heat-sensitive, they lose their value if faced with temperature above forty-five degrees Celsius. Thanks to enzymes, cells constantly regenerate, and that regeneration is the foundation of life.

"Health is not valued until sickness comes." -Thomas Fuller

2.How to Gulp Your Way to Evolution

My father started looking into the issue of water. He researched the results of studies and found out that getting high-quality water is not easy these days. Although tap water is cleaned through filters, just like bottled water, it is contaminated with gases, chloride, fluoride, hormones, heavy metals and bacteria, all of which soak through earth from waste water and often infiltrate clean, already filtered water.

My father started testing his water and read books by a Japanese researcher, Dr. Masaru Emoto. He froze distilled water to get it to resemble the structure of an ice molecule with the ideal crystal grid. When the water melted, it had the same qualities as the water of our ancestors. My mom drank dad's modified water daily. My father continued to study, moving on to the principle of filtering water through reverse osmosis, and through this method he eliminated ninety percent of harmful additions, ending up with chemical-free water that he enriched with calcium and magnesium. He installed the filtering device underneath the kitchen sink and made it possible for my mother to get a cup of truly clean water by simply turning the water tap. Today, my parents use the latest filtering machine running on the principle of electrolysis. No person in our household drinks anything but alkaline water. These new arrangements helped my mother and the whole family establish and maintain a drinking regime. Unfortunately, before doing so, none of us drank much water. First, we built the habit of drinking a full glass after waking up, giving the body an opportunity to quickly get rid of the toxins that had gathered during sleep. The path to eliminating toxins is fairly straightforward: to get toxins out of the body, I must drink enough water that will carry them out through the kidneys, sweat, etc. We introduced another new tactic of not drinking thirty minutes before and after our meals to avoid lowering the absorption of food nutrients by the body. Drinking three liters of water daily became our minimal goal. Amongst other things, my mother got rid of her lifelong constipation, and my father's blood pressure fell to healthy levels. My dad supported my mom as much as he could, but he refused to even taste the green drink she made daily. He called it Swampwater. My mother made it by blending alkaline water with either clover, alfalfa, or other green herbs she harvested. After five minutes of blending, she let the mixture sit in the refrigerator for one hour, and then filtered it through cloth and drank it. Chlorophyll, the most effective ingredient of the green drink, has a chemical structure similar to that of an oxygen-transporting metalloprotein called hemoglobin. Aside from vitamins, enzymes, minerals, biologically active materials, and disinfecting and healing effects, it also includes healing energy from the sun. Swampwater was my mother's daily strong alkalizing drink.

3.How to Survive "White Poisons"

Mother eliminated acid-forming red meat, chicken, and fish from her diet. She also started exercising regularly, took walks in nature, and strolled by lakes and through forests to provide her cells with oxygen. Exercising oxygenates the human organism, and that is a very important thing. Inside a body with enough oxygen and alkalinity, a cancer or any other sickness cannot survive.

Both of us committed to serious changes in dietary habits. We hung lists of alkalizing and acidizing food in the kitchen and strictly followed them. An American doctor by the name of Robert Morse suggested that sources of all illness are either acidity or toxicity of foods, air, cleaning products, building materials, and the living environment. Because I wanted to support my mother all the way, I only ate what she ate. Our biggest issue was giving up white poisons, as Dr. Walker labeled milk, sugar, flour and salt.

I heard about the harmful effects of cow milk on the human body many years ago, but I entered a state of shock when I found out online about a spreading inflammation of udders in farm cows. The news story announced that one liter of milk contained four million cells of pus. This resulted in us drinking the antibiotics these cows received as their lifelong treatment. Casein is a protein found abundantly in cow's milk, its high concentration is responsible for creating abnormal amounts of mucus in the body. Casein is also a substance commonly used as reliable glue popular amongst carpenters. Yogurts are some of the most chemically altered milk products. If yogurts with the word Bio on their labels truly contained live cultures, their tops would explode inside the refrigerator within one day. Isn't it suspicious that yogurt can remain unspoiled for up to three months? We decided to leave cow milk to calves, which were, after all, meant to have it anyway, and thus we stopped filling our bodies with mucus. We replaced cow milk with almond milk. Before this change, we filled our bodies with outrageous amounts of acids by consuming milk products. To maintain balanced levels of pH, our blood removed calcium from bones, muscles and teeth, and so, along with filling our bodies with toxins, we also lost much-needed calcium. My mother couldn't believe she forced me to eat yogurt and cheese when I was a little girl, thinking these products would strengthen my teeth and bones.

Our family absolutely loved homemade white bread, cakes

and other foods my mother made based on my grandmother's recipes. It was difficult for her to say goodbye to white flour, but the fact is that despite high precautions, flour storage silos are frequently infiltrated by mold. Ground flour contains gluten, a protein composite known for damaging the liver, pancreas, and intestines. What more, our test strips showed that foods containing flour significantly raised our urine acidity.

Only whole grains in their natural state are alkaline. My mother soaked whole grains of buckwheat and wheat, then blended them with honey, raisins, unsweetened coconut, cinnamon and warm water to create a delicious, white flour-free dessert.

We learned that legumes, such as lentils, beans and peas, need to be soaked for at least 48 hours. This is because their natural toxins mother nature equipped them with to deal with pests. The toxins were flushed out by the long soaking and the briefly cooked legumes were ready for consumption.

Breaking News: It takes the body two days to process one teaspoon of sugar! Cancer cells love refined sugar, and nothing supported their growth more than the eating of sugar. All types of sugar foster the growth of cancerous cells, including brown sugar, so-called organic sugar, syrups, everything sweetened by sugar. A decision was made. The only sugars we were allowed to eat from then on were reasonable amounts of fructose in fruits, quality honey, agave, stevia and maple syrup in small amounts. Artificial sweeteners are completely unacceptable, too!

Members of certain Native American and Eskimo tribes never ate salt and lived in good health. After studying nutritional labels, I was horrified by the amounts of salt added into bread, processed meats and canned foods. The only part of salt necessary for a human being is organic chlorine, which can be reliably replaced with celery juice. Dr. Walker asserted that salt tends to mummify living organisms, examples being the graying of hair, skin shrinkage, rheumatism, overload of kidneys, and high blood pressure. All the salt we need is contained in fruits and vegetables.

Vegetable and animal oils previously used for cooking, ended up in the trashcans of our households. Fat from these oils does not breakdown inside the body, instead plugging up capillaries, blocking the supply of oxygen, and thus causing what we call dead cells. Dead cells acidize their surroundings, turning healthy cells malignant. Unhealthy fats are one of the frequent causes of breast and intestinal cancers. We kept only our flaxseed oil, stored in the fridge for special opportunities, and the versatile coconut oil. Along with culinary pursuits, the latter served us well as a skincare product for the whole body, excellent toothpaste, and effective furniture polish.

My mother and I ate the simplest foods and chewed them for as long as possible. Well-chewed foods provided the body with even more regenerating nourishment. The oral cavity is an exclusive provider of specific enzymes that are irreplaceable in the grand scheme of human digestion.

We took two hour breaks between different types of foods to make sure they wouldn't mix within the stomach, ferment, and cause increased acidity. We ate fruit an hour before or after other meals because it ferments with any other type of food. Divided nourishment is ideal for healthy digestion. There are many websites full of tips and recipes on how to properly divide, combine and prepare different food groups. The main step at the beginning was to separate every grown food, i.e. plants, from animal foods. Later we found out that vegetable salads can be mixed with anything, but fruits should be consumed separately, watermelon is best not combined with any fruits, and bananas should be the last fruit eaten. Meat and sides shouldn't be combined, just as animal products such as cheese, milk, and yogurt don't mix well with baked goods and any plant foods. Neutral foods like raisins, honey, poppy, and almonds can be eaten with anything. Eskimos have come to benefit greatly from thusly divided eating, because although they have always been meat eaters, cancer amongst their population is rare. This is because they don't eat much sugar. In comparison, Indians love sugar, but their cancer rates are also low. This is because they eat less meat. People elsewhere, it seems, think it is a good idea to eat potato fries with fried chicken and sweet ketchup on regular basis.

My parents and I stuffed ourselves with fruits and vegetables rich in vitamins and minerals, homemade juices without sugar, soaked grains, seeds, nuts and dried fruits. I had no idea that tomatoes belonged in the fruit group and though they are alkaline in their raw form, heat preparation turns them into an acidified bomb inside the human body. Eating ketchup means filling one's body with acids because this sweetened, cooked, acidified, chemically colored, preservative-filled mixture is not food, but poison.

We strictly excluded processed foods with coloring additions, artificial sweeteners, and conservatives, along with genetically modified goods, coffee and alcohol. Beer and wine do count as alcohol. Baking, harmful cooking, frying and grilling also stopped existing for us, because through these methods we destroyed most nutritional benefits of the modified food, and frying causes side chemical reactions that result in toxins.

We threw away our dangerous microwave. Not only does it erase nutritional value of foods and removes life energy, but it damages the human body by radiation even when it isn't turned on. It is the same type of radiation emitting from cell phones and computers. The biggest danger of the microwave lies in carcinogen effects of accumulated radiation. Professor P. Brodeur said that Microwave radiation has dangerous culminating effects, and the food prepared in a microwave oven becomes a carrier of radiation. The changes in exposed blood are immediately visible. The human immune system, however, does not react with the usual defense mechanisms, and a blood sample analysis shows us cancer in progress. Microwaves are a more frequent cause of cancer than smoking. Children do not have this information, cannot defend themselves, and so their health is in the hands of adults. Items like plastic containers, plastic wrappers, and foil don't belong in the microwave. Neither does any type of paper that can be soaked, as it can absorb the cancerous dioxins released when food is heated inside of plastic. Plastic water bottles left in the car during high temperatures are equally deadly.

We did our best to avoid the poisonous fluoride, a frequent additive in water and toothpaste. Fluoride is necessary for life, but only in small amounts, as proven by its small presence in breast milk. Constant intake of fluoride is dangerous for human brain cells and overall mental and physical health. Latest research shows that fluoride damages the brain and lowers children's IQ. It's impossible for me to understand why it would be added into our children's food, citrus drinks and juices. Tons of fluorides were used in the atomic industry to enrich uranium, just as they were used by pharmaceutical manufacturers to make fertilizer and pesticide. Through the fertilizer, fluoride thus contaminated the soil, food and water. The USA government banned its usage in drinking water. Hitler used fluoride in concentration camp liquidations. It also served well as rat poison.

4.Spiritual Sandwich

We integrated all of these changes into our daily routines and worked hard to de-acidify our bodies and give any kind of virus, bacteria or cancer cell no chance to survive. My mother whipped a mixture of hot water, a few teaspoons of natural maple syrup and baking soda into a compact foam, which she enjoyed a couple of times a day. She believed that this mixture, popularized by an American healer Jim Kelmun, effectively kills carcinogenic cells and thus functions as natural chemotherapy without side effects. According to his Protocol, molecules of baking soda and maple syrup bond together and create modified glucose that is absorbed by the carcinogenic cells, as these cells love sugar. The baking soda that the glucose sneakily smuggles into the cells raises their pH and destroys them before they can perform cell division. Simply put, cancer cannot survive in an alkaline environment. The theory of anti-cancerous effects of peach kernel is based on a similar principle, as these kernels contain small amounts of poisonous cyanide that can kill the cells from within. My mother ground a few of these kernels every day and sprinkled them on her salads. Edward Griffin's book, titled "World without Cancer," describes his observation of a small Asian tribe whose people never died of cancer and regularly lived to be a hundred. He noted that they regularly consumed peaches, kernels included. A former director of the US National Institute for Cancer Research, Dr. Dean Burk, dedicated forty-five years of his life to cancer studies, specifically the anti-cancer effects of the vitamin B-17, a substance contained, amongst other foods, inside peach kernels. Dr. Burk publicly confirmed that that its benefits were proven by clinical research across the United States and he himself considered it the most effective form of cancer treatment he had encountered during his studies. The kernels must be eaten in small doses and intake is raised slowly. My mom ate around ten kernels per day shortly after her cancer was discovered.

My mother the patient also followed the advice of Dr. Joseph Mercola and filled her body with sufficient amounts of vitamin D3, in health crisis over 10,000 IU, in form of orally absorbed pills. The body can create vitamin D3 with enough supply of sunlight. Mercola recommends at least some daily contact with the sun to give our organism an opportunity to develop the vitamin. Of course, this becomes a challenge for people living in areas with small amounts of sunshine. Research conducted by Harvard

University confirmed that people with high amount of vitamin D don't suffer from cancer, and vitamin D is the best cancer vaccine. Doctor Joseph Mercola warns that vitamin D and vitamin A shouldn't be consumed together because it will numb their effects. This is the reason multivitamins are often ineffective, because the effects of their contents can cancel each other out. An oil contained in cod liver, retinol, can completely eliminate the effects of vitamin D. Both vitamins can be found in sufficient amounts within red fruits and vegetables. Everyday supply of 300mg of magnesium and 400mg of vitamin E is necessary for prevention and treatment of breast cancer, as is the monitoring of hormonal balance, especially for women over forty. Doctors still prescribe estrogen to women of this age, but many medical journals have published articles suggesting that estrogen overload can lead to uterine cancer. The progressive Dr. Mercola stresses the importance of higher intake of progesterone, a hormone that lowers the cancer risk. His recommendation, however, only applies to natural progesterone, and he completely rejects its artificially created form.

Mom also experimented with methods prescribed by Dr. Johana Budwig, who has been nominated for the Nobel prize seven times for "healing through food," treatment during which she served her terminally ill patients flaxseed oil, rich in Omega3 oils, and organic cottage cheese and yogurt containing high quality protein. Some of the patients only had hours to live when the treatment started, and survived. We also became fond of goat milk products. Goats are very picky about their nutrition, and they would certainly not touch anything filled with chemicals. Dr. Budwig recommended frequent contact with nature and the beneficial effects of the sun, which shines on us through tree leaves colored by chlorophyll. People with highly acidified bodies frequently felt ill and suffered burned skin when exposed to the sun, but after alkalization, these problems disappeared.

I remember when mom met a nurse with breast cancer on one of the forums she frequented. Anna worked in a hospital and didn't care for alternative healing methods. She never found the courage to rely on them, choosing instead of undergo lengthy chemotherapy and regular treatment. The time after her death was very difficult for my mother.

Another woman my mom met on the internet, Ema, was twenty years older than her and had healthy doses of determination. Ema found a doctor who diagnosed with a specialized machine measuring the frequencies of individual organs. It's a method of diagnosis based on the fact that each organ has its own frequency of bioenergy, and if the organ isn't functioning properly, the frequency changes accordingly to the level of dysfunction. Another machine, invented by Dr. Clark, then destroys pathogens with directed, tumor-specific electric frequencies. Dr. Hulda Clark considered parasites, viruses, bacteria and fungi to be the cause of all illnesses, cancer included. According to her research, we all have parasites inside our bodies without being actively aware of them. These uninvited guests can be microscopic, but also grow to the size of few meters inside of the intestines. Parasites can live in our muscles, eyes, skin and brains. According to Dr. Clark, most parasites infiltrate the organism through meat, hot dogs, ham, hamburgers and fish. She considers a parasite by the name of common intestinal fluke to be the so-called "cancer specialist". Its eggs make it to the body through unwashed vegetables, fruits, and domestic pets. Another widely spread parasite is yeast – over ninety percent of the human population is supposedly affected. An effective yeast killer is coconut oil, thanks to the caprylic acid it contains. An extract from the American walnut tree, prepared in accordance with Dr. Clark's original recipe, has the ability to cleanse the intestines of all parasites. Ema went to have her intestines flushed out more frequently than she visited her hairstylist, and underwent exhausting cleansings of the liver and kidneys. While undergoing this detox crisis, as her body eliminated decades' worth of sediments and she felt consistently ill, she never stopped joking and laughing. She knew very well that intestinal cleansing was a necessity for her, given she had lung cancer and the intestines and lungs are paired organs. Often it is sufficient to heal the paired organ for the other to recover. Ema claims that information she found in the book of Dr. Walker, whom is nicknamed "The Juiceman," saved her life.

My friend Nancy called me one day to let me know she was diagnosed with stomach cancer and her doctor insisted on chemotherapy. She was crushed and resigned. I advised her to buy Dr. Walker's thin books. She read them in a flash and devised a battle plan according to his instructions. Her doctor was shocked and couldn't believe her test results. She gave him Walker's books to study. To this day, Nancy advises people with serious illnesses, shares her stories with a wide audience and invests her money into purchasing hundreds of Dr. Walker's books. She hands them out to patients in oncology departments for free.

Mother's typical daily menu before she got sick:

Breakfast

White roll with butter, cow milk with cocoa and sugar.

Morning snack

White bread, spreadable cheese, lunchmeat.

Lunch

Beef broth with noodles, dumplings, cream sauce, pork.

Afternoon snack

Cheese pie with preserves, black coffee with whipped cream.

Dinner

Fried cheese, French fries, mayo.

Mother's new menu, from the beginning of her treatment until now:

Breakfast

Fresh homemade apple juice.

Morning snack

Fruit.

Lunch

Steamed vegetables, whole grain brown rice, plantains fried with coconut oil.

Afternoon snack

Barley coffee, almond milk, bananas.

Dinner

Veggie salad.

"Let food be thy medicine and your medicine be thy food."

-Greek Proverb

We won the battle. My mother cured her cancer and has been healthy and active for years.

There is nothing else to add.

5.Reality Maker

What did the illness mean to my mother? Was it a way for her to learn so many new things and consciously change her lifestyle and point of view? Why didn't we learn all of this in school? How is it possible that we need cancer to make us realize basic facts about food, about the functions of our bodies and causes of sickness? Where did things go wrong? Why didn't we see earlier how we ruined our health with food? How is it possible that Hypocrites would tell my mother to fast and give her an enema after the operation, but the hospital doctors let her have fried potatoes and schnitzel? How can it be legal to serve chocolate without cocoa, lunchmeats containing cancerous nitrite E250, cheese that isn't really cheese or strawberry yogurt without strawberries, miraculously long-lasting milk that can stay open in the fridge for five months without spoiling?

I still don't understand why modern medicine only focuses on easing pain and curing the symptoms of illnesses. The most important thing – the cause for sickness – is swept under the rug and ignored. Animals living in the wild don't consume pills, and thus don't have ruined liver and kidneys.

Humans cannot even imagine living without pills. But if we were to practically combine medical discoveries with nature's abilities, we could eliminate illness and completely regenerate the human body.

The commonly reported findings about cholesterol are also fraudulent. While studying the articles about food alkalinity, I encountered trivial information stating that whenever inflammation arises within the body, cholesterol grows with it. When we eliminate inflammation, cholesterol levels fall. Because inflammation doesn't happen inside of an alkaline body, keeping our pH on or above the level of seven will ensure we won't struggle with cholesterol.

"*Nearly all men die of their remedies and not of their illnesses.*"
-Moliere

If I look at this situation through the eyes of those we allow to manipulate us, meaning moneygrubbers and politicians who are manipulated by even more powerful individuals going all the way to the top few, things become clear. Enlightenment, good health, knowledge and truth do not increase profits. Illness, blind faith, addiction and ignorance are, however, extremely lucrative commodities.

To illustrate, I'll present the case of an average small European state, let's name it XY, with the population of ten million people. A conscientious citizen of such country would attempt to lower the country's national debt and bring money to small businesses. There are many ways to do that. Let's say his monthly wage is 8,000 Euros, and every month he pays 2,000 Euros in income taxes and 500 Euros in healthcare taxes. His employer puts another 1,600 Euros into the country's treasure chest. Our citizen eats 240 kilograms of meat every year! By doing so, he gives the government 250 Euros and increases his chance of early death by cancer or heart disease, thus not living long enough to collect pension. Citizen of the state XY will drink twenty-four beers and a bottle of whiskey every week. He pays the state 610 Euros yearly by doing so. An ideal citizen must smoke two packs of cigarettes daily. This will make the state richer by 1,500 Euros, and the dedicated citizen will, in thirteen years, increase his chance of early death by lung cancer fifty times. If he drives his car for around six thousand miles, he'll bring the state 9,540 Euros. His family of five will give the government 4,000 Euros in taxes for groceries and medication. Country XY pays a few more billions into pension security than it collects. The ideal citizen tries to relieve the state's burden and sacrifices his health by avoiding visits to the doctor. He dies when he is 62, exactly on the day when he was supposed to start collecting pension.

Can you imagine what the statistics are for bigger countries? Do you see how absurd all of it is? Why do we support it? If we made real health a priority, we'd make millions of doctors, the pharmaceutical industry, the food industry, agricultural industry, slaughterhouses and people who trade human health and suffering much, much poorer.

"Even a blind horse can run on a straight road."
-European proverb

My mother and I never wanted to leave the new lifestyle we built. On the contrary, it fulfills us and makes us both permanently happy. I'm relieved I was able to cleanse my body from the toxic particles I gathered from the air, food, water, and chemical leftovers of everything I collected in my body throughout my life. I underwent the uncomfortable detox of my organism - effects of which included acne and aching nodes, joints, head and back – and arrived at a feeling of perfect health and satisfaction.

6.Active Ignorance Free

One advantage I had in this process was my refusal to eat red meat, fish and poultry since I was twenty years old. I considered this to be an important decision not only for humanitarian reason, but because of ethical issues and health benefits. My significant vegetarian role models were Plato, Socrates, Seneca, Leonardo da Vinci, Benjamin Franklin, Isaac Newton, Henry Ford, Gandhi, and others. According to scientific research, humans were originally herbivores, collecting and consuming fruits, veggies, nuts and seeds. Intestines of herbivores are typically a few meters long. Thanks to their stomach enzymes, cows can digest food for longer before it passes through their four-stomach digestive tract. Logically we can deduce that meat would rot were it inside the intestines for that long. This decay would create toxic elements and cause illness. Humans too have very long intestines, a sufficient proof we were meant to digest plant food. Wild predators, however, have extraordinarily developed liver and short intestines, thus the meat toxins can pass through quickly and these animals can digest without any complications.

Cows and horses never ate meat and never went to school, yet they've always respected their intestinal equipment designed exclusively for herbivores. Have you ever seen elephants, rhinoceros, heifers or giraffes eat meat? You haven't. They belong amongst the biggest and strongest animals in the world, yet they eat plant food and never feel weak. Just as well, you can't force a lion to graze on a grass pasture. Let's not even get into the horrible documentaries capturing the awful conditions of slaughterhouse animals, and their treatment before and during slaughter. In the past, I hadn't considered that animals can sense death and their fear causes adrenalin to flood their muscles; muscles that are later consumed by humans. I realized this is why people consuming meat have been extremely aggressive and violent throughout human history. One more thing... Have you ever looked deeply into the eyes of a calf? You would be surprised by what you'd see there.

Many "experts" claim that people need meat because of its significant amounts of protein. They tend to omit that since meat is not meant to be the source of protein for humans, the body can only process it at a great cost in energy, because it must first turn meat into an amino-acid before building a useful protein. Many people feel tired after eating meat because all of their energy is spent on protein fission. I'm not sure why experts don't write about the amino-acids readily contained in vegetables, and the fact that the body can simply create proteins from them without the demanding fission. Misinformation is often created by taking sentences out of context and making it seem like there aren't any other choices in the matter.

Some of my friend attempted to crash my vegetarian convictions by arguing that the plants I eat also had to be removed from existence. I tried to explain to them that plants belong into a lower biological category and most of them had given us their fruits and lived on. Other plants left their seeds behind to ensure continuation, thus surviving in their own way.

For the past few years since my mother's illness, I've been a vegan. I don't eat anything that comes from animals, and no cooked or otherwise heat-prepared foods – raw food only. My switch from cooked vegetarian diet to a raw vegan diet was accompanied by an incredible boost in my overall health. I searched for an expert explanation of this phenomenon, and found that due to cooked, fried, baked and otherwise nutrient-stripped foods, my blood was thicker than the lymph liquid, as was therefore unable to carry toxins out of my body, allowing them instead to settle in tissue. That is why I occasionally experienced stiffness and lack of flexibility. It is also one of the causes for accelerated aging. Though a raw diet, the blood thinned to its healthy form and the toxins were flushed from blood into the lymph nodes, which then carried them into the liver and kidneys.

"We are what we eat." –Hippocrates

7.Common Sense Movement

It's absurd that it took a serious illness of a loved one to teach me how to eat correctly and take care of my body. It was probably the only bulletproof way life could shake me out of my stupor and shine some light on a new path. Before, my life resembled drunken surfing on a banana peel. Whenever I managed to crawl out of the water, a new wave crashed into me and I slipped on a new peel. I set on a course of balance and harmony, the two things I didn't know much about before. Balancing my life was never a skill I possessed or knew how to implement into everyday life. I had much to learn, and veganism helped me get there. I disconnected myself from the herds of blind believers frequenting diners, buffets and restaurants; those who spend money at grocery stores for poisons they slowly but surely kill themselves with at home. My revelation went even further. I began to receive flows of energy and understood that along with regeneration, cleansing and healing of my physical body, I also finally knew how to use the piles of gathered spiritual information I mentioned at the beginning. I managed to open the gate to true spirituality and felt how incredibly interconnected all things are. Many may consider this hard to believe, but it was the energy from living nutrition that opened my ability for higher perception. Without the physical progress, I would never have found true spirituality. By the way, one can successfully surf even on top of a banana peel, as long as we remember to always keep balance.

"*One should not treat the eye without the head, head without the body, and the body without a soul.*" -Hippocrates

I stopped worrying about things I couldn't change and accepted life as it happened. It sounds simple enough, but it was nearly an impossible task for an Aries. I searched for nature subconsciously and automatically received its energy, the same kind of energy I obtained from raw foods and daily exercise. I learned to forgive. I simply let any slights or insults go. When someone hurt me, I didn't forget and didn't excuse their action, but I chose to leave it behind and never return to it. I adjusted myself to it, but I didn't burn a bridge to the future, where a new chance could await. It was not for me to judge and punish. To flee from the reach of bad energy was, however, necessary. It's good for us to keep up our borders, establish some limits for people and refuse access. Every wrong act attracts through its own energy similar vibrations and their initiator will feel them. To forgive others is to allow oneself to access the foundation of personal cleansing. With a weak inner harmony, we are more open to dark influences that only understand these negative vibrations and attach themselves like big juicy flies onto a flytrap.

My main mission was to do my BEST while performing any task, minor or major, pleasurable or unpleasant. I knew that humans don't create good and evil, only conditions to invite one or the other. What mattered was the point of view we chose to adopt. I had a choice to welcome each day with a tongue tasting of vinegar or honey. Whether I should spend twenty-four hours causing problems and bad blood, performing bad work, hurting others, complaining, or doing the best I could with what I had was purely my choice.

"*I've had a lot of worries in my life, most of which never happened.*"
-Mark Twain

I tried to create a nourishing environment for good and positive thoughts, feelings and wishes. The opposite forces of good and evil have been battling each other since ancient epics and fairy tales. They could never co-exist, just like one cannot be simultaneously single and married. Good and evil are two different coins, two different realities. They are not like day and night or rise and fall of tides, but rather phenomena that do not fight each other but peacefully take turns at regular intervals.

Creating a positive life was and is an incredible experience. I witnessed how good and evil work and confirmed that the laws of cause and effect were just in each case. When I objectively searched through my conscience, I could find the probable consequences following my missteps, payback in form of bad luck, financial loss, illness, and other punches. For my good deeds I was rewarded with wonderful people and beneficial situations. I was never naïve enough to believe that one can only fight evil with good. I also wasn't of the opinion that evil should be punished with evil. Wise people always stood against evil, but punishment is unnecessary. Negative energy will always turn against its evil initiator.

"*To wish to be well is part of becoming well.*" -Lucius Seneca

8.Simple Complexology

I found increasingly more strength and relief. I regained common sense, and by that I mean the natural and comfortable ability to make decisions without exaggerated searching, thinking and contemplating. I felt fantastic eating raw food that energized my body and mind. The energy I suddenly had at my disposal helped me see things clearly.

It seems I was supposed to spend the first twenty years of my life as a skeptical materialist, the next twenty a spiritually-oriented seeker, only to realize by age forty that either of the extremes doesn't work as well as both of them combined. I realized that neither of the two, materialist or idealist, can ever achieve anything beyond the top level of materialism or idealism. This one-sided race prevents many from actual personal enrichment.

To focus only on gathering possessions, building a career and finding happiness in owning things, often on the expense of others, always felt brainless and emotionless to me. I was convinced that human existence is not limited to a single life and doesn't come randomly, as Darwin claimed. After all, there is no proof for this widely spread theory, and we've never discovered all the supposed links of development from one species to another, suggested by Darwin. Though this theory is routinely taught in schools, no one has provided proof of its validity. Luckily, thanks to much scientific research and logical conclusions, many scientists find themselves attracted to a theory of evolutionary development that happened separately with each species. In other words, everything didn't come from one, but different types of species that developed separately.

"*Darwinism isn't even a theory, but coincidence which had captured the minds of men. It's science as much as fairy tale is a history book.*" -Albert Wigand

To find common truth, I used my senses, sight, hearing, touch, taste and smell, just as my parents taught me when I was little. But my senses were often tricked by cleverly masked lies. After all, millions of people in the past and present time have been fooled by TV commercials, news stories with biases and spins, information taken out of context, and flattering rhetoric of extremely gifted speakers fooling those with blind faith. I had to admit that faith and reason were easily confused. Not even science could always answer all of my questions, and couldn't step behind the borders of the spiritual to explain certain occurrences. People focused exclusively on the material always had a tendency to put too much stock in reason and suppress emotional intuition, and thus they were affected only by prejudices, opinions of the majority, conventional approaches and relationships. A typical sign of the stubborn old school of science is the sentence its proponents use when they're out of arguments: "What cannot be measured does not exist." Often, when I tried to offer some spiritually-minded information to one of these materialistic skeptics, they silenced me or called me crazy. Materialists functioning on this frequency can only accept information given to them on that same frequency. But just because they rejected the spiritual part of the world didn't mean they weren't affected by its forces. Such skeptic will not wake in this life, not until faced with serious illness that will force him to obtain new information and open his mind to life's mysteries.

"*It's very depressing to live in a time where it's easier to break an atom than a prejudice.*" -Albert Einstein

Naturally, I pondered how else to find the real, 100% accurate truth. Leave the firm ground under my feet, distance myself from responsibility, give up my possessions, live in poverty because "I am above owning material objects, money, caring about my body." It felt illogical and absurd to be born in a material world and wait all of my life for the moment I could leave it behind, rise into higher spheres and hope I could find something extraordinary there to keep me from coming back.

What would be the point? Many of my friends and acquaintances found themselves on a certain level of spiritual development and, sometimes fanatically, refused to acknowledge any new opinions or information. They got themselves stuck halfway. I was happy that my one-sided spiritual journey didn't lead me to this incredible bitterness, as it led them.

There was a time in my life when I was fascinated by spiritual teachers and people who spent time around spiritual seminars and esoteric books, or published about these topics online. Even then, however, I felt an important thing was missing, the esoteric principle, a strange thing to become absent from spiritual leaders. Should they charge money for help? Shouldn't a healer wait to see if the patient will reward him with money or other gifts, subject to that person's situation? Was the spiritual sphere meant for gold diggers and businessmen? Were the propagators of spirituality supposed to make lots of money, or rather perform a service to the public? Isn't the constant stream of equal taking and giving one of the basic rules of natural prosperity? From where and by what right did they gather energy to perform acts of magic?

An individual performed different forms of energy manipulation with her own conscience and will, and it didn't matter whether the person believed she was practicing magic or not. All of those who used energy taken from someone or something to reach their goals engaged in manipulation. Every magician operated on the same basis of manipulation. There isn't a big difference between magic and manipulation. With every act of manipulation, the person purposely degraded both the living and non-living subjects into items and placed them wherever he desired, did with them as she pleased. For example, whenever a woman emphasized her physical attractiveness, she manipulated the thought process of a man. When a magician, shaman or sorcerer called upon the power of fire to force a man to notice the woman, it was magic. Both methods used something to influence someone. Human beings have been familiar with the temptation of manipulation throughout history in form of favoritism, bribery, even using God to enforce obedience and submission. Another method of magic was the control over the faith of human beings, practiced by all world religions. During the medieval ages, the Catholic Church tortured and burned witches, and free will was not really known to humans until the dawn of capitalism. Amongst the modern tools of control over our minds are alcohol, tobacco, drugs, food, video games and television.

The entire world was controlled by a small group of people, masters of manipulation who would, for example, keep scientific discoveries from the eyes of the public. They refused to publicize the possibilities of unlimited energy sources, manipulated secret databases containing personal data, and twisted inconvenient truths with the help of mass communication tools.

This manipulation was sophisticated and difficult to uncover. It easily fooled the human senses, because humans are attracted to shine, a good show, superficial brilliance, fabulous disguises and masks of promising words, shards of nonsense that deflected attention whenever necessary. And that's how people exchanged the needed, the useful and the natural for harmful pretense and lies, often while their will was good. The bigger the lack of knowledge in a person was, the easier it was to manipulate them. Television, media and books belonged and still belong amongst the number one tools of mass control over our minds.

Lately, one of the most popular methods of practice has become "spirituality of all kinds," and one of the most popular branches of this movement has been witchcraft. After all, magic always offered a guaranteed and quick resolve. To many people, it brought tragic life problems as a penalty to pay for this artificial interference with the flow of life. Numerous entities with the intention of binding themselves onto the person and causing them harm became one with the energy of dark magic. Magic used the elements of water, air, earth and fire, summoning them violently and using their extra-physical entities to influence love, health, luck, beauty and power. I knew a woman who used the power of fire summoned during a ritual to attract the man she loved. After some time, she married him, and soon her life became unbearable. The new husband humiliated and abused her until she committed suicide. The fire energy released during rituals was historically connected to the negative energy of Spanish Inquisition, and these dark entities likely entered the woman's life, causing her to lose control. After the initial result and fulfillment of her wish, she faced an opposite effect and a heavy punishment. This was one of the main principles of magic functioning in practical life, but many other hidden principles exist. If a person was connected to magic, they would become a part of its negative influence regardless of the purity of their intent. Even the use of magically influenced "charmed" ring, cross, necklace, bracelet, herbs, potion, ointment, picture, or Tarot cards was, in its essence, manipulation. Same with rituals, magic symbols, magically influenced music, drugs, hallucinogenic mushrooms, methods of deep regression, holotropic breathing methods, repetition of prayers and mantras, fortification of the ego, visualization, spiritual communication with ghosts etc…these were all nothing but tools of manipulation with unnatural paths. The practice of magic was then always a short loan with high interest rate, and too many people paid dearly. It could never truly help humanity and push it toward real progress. I do not mean to judge or criticize, only to objectively point out the results of known history. If these spiritual paths and systems were successful, they would not have led us to the indifference with which we tolerate extinctions of entire animal species and look on as the planet's natural resources are irreversibly depleted, air poisoned, water contaminated. On the contrary – if these methods had worked, we would be respectful and protective of Mother Nature and our Earth.

The so-called Mystical path of spreading love also belonged to the category of artificial interference. It was perhaps never natural to purposely spread love in the first place. Love spread itself. Love was or was not present on its own, independent of will and desire. True love was, is and always will be a result, not a condition. How would a sentence like "I willed myself to love" sound? What brought a mother to love her child? Nothing. Her love rose from the depths of her core without any need for meddling. If love came about by calculation, it wasn't love.

Unstoppable consumption of chaotic information, visits to seminars, or webpages about spiritual matters were not sufficient resources, because not all of them were truthful and dependable, not all could be accepted by the seeker. During my own "magic phase," I felt signs of addiction flavored with a pinch of fanaticism, the desire to fight violently for my own convictions instead of considering a different path. I wasn't willing to accept even for a second the smallest hint of criticism. I was so powerfully motivated by practicing paths that led to nowhere.

Magic was created as a link on the path of human development, one that has to be left behind at a certain point. That's how I see things now, and I know that only without it I can reach the next step in my evolution, the place of balance, harmony, and synergy with nature. Why do the manipulators support the modern wave of spiritualism and magic, everything summarized under the label 'New Age'? They do it because it's attractive, mysterious, guaranteed, promises answers to many questions, and produces just the right amount of addiction to help control a herd of sheep. It does not, however, consider the matters of true purpose, needs and functions of the physical body, its balance and harmony.

This reoccurring group of few powerful individuals who tug at world's strings and determine its rules knows very well that our physical bodies could, on this Earth, achieve a perfect harmony with spiritual bodies and, with proper care and communication, show us the real way to the impulses of nature and the universe. Their energy could flow from us automatically, without outside interruptions, and bring us knowledge which is now hidden or only shown through brief flashes. This natural way of energy reception functions through body care, daily exercise, raw diet, contact with nature, and elimination of negative influences. A path of everyday routine is the only path that leads to an evolutionary step forward. Manipulators would lose influence and control. It's the reason why people have been purposely misinformed for centuries, and whenever a piece of real knowledge made it through into someone's mind, most were too lazy to try to understand it and instead chose the method of "do it for me, magician, do it faster and without effort on my part." After all, it is more fun to play with magical cards than to sweat every day during exercise and take the time to make juices and salads at home.

"*Love comes when manipulation stops.*" -Dr. Joyce Brothers

Magical practices didn't manage to protect and help the humankind, as demonstrated by the devastated state of our environment, global famine, poverty, war, and other evils. Isn't this enough of a proof that methods of manipulation do not work? That it's time to try something different? Isn't it our duty to find the next step in our evolution and save the planet? The fact is, magic and other spiritual endeavors did not lead humans to evolution. It is time to change our approach, stop manipulating, and try something that was not affected by negative energy in the past. Turn to nature. Instead of abusing it, robbing it, exterminating it, we should become a part of it and defend its riches instead of stealing them. We could behave more like the Iroquois, a Native American tribe whose members cared for the well-being of their seventh generation as much as they cared for their own. The rule of the seventh generation is still alive within some current environmental preservation movements. If we can become one with nature, understand its language, tune ourselves to its frequency, then we can gather the information needed to take another step as a species on this planet. I believe that we weren't given our physical form randomly, but so we could join forces with spiritual bodies and make significant progress in the material world. When the physical shell is destroyed after death, our spiritual presence cannot take any further step in the evolutionary process. It has to wait for another body in a waiting room where not much happens. It was paradoxical, but it was the convictions I held with such dedication, my obsession with teachings of spiritual guides and their books, that prevented me from moving forward for so long. For example, I reached the highest skill of Tarot card readings, but I was entirely dependent on the established system and what each card told me. I felt I needed a change. I threw numerous boxes filled with accessories for magic, symbols, cards, CDs and spiritual books into the garbage can.

The time before my "New Era" was over. I entered the present day. I'm relieved, and I know where to go and how to get there. I'm beginning to count the days of My New Era.

PART TWO

SymBioEra

Day One of My New Era

Whenever I look inside a spiritual or religious book, I find out that the center of our spiritual life resides inside the body in form of a soul, and the physical body around it is its shield, defense, shell. When the books include information about an active light surrounding the physical body, they describe it as glow coming from the soul and shining through and outside of the body. The soul allegedly only has one goal, to escape the body and reach higher spheres and dimensions. Many religions speak about the end of earthly suffering and the soul freeing itself of the pesky shell.

Why, then, do we have a body made of flesh and bones? How is it possible that this spiritually neglected outer shell was the one reliable thing that led me to true spirituality? Why do we live in a material world? What is this difficult, complicated life for? What is the purpose of life on Earth? The answer is obvious and logical. It is here on Earth, inside our physical bodies, we're supposed make the evolutionary step forward! Only here we can truly learn. One lifetime is like a single day in school. We must return many times to finish our studies. After fulfilling all degree requirements, we can finally get some answers.

A theory I find to be much more logical is that of a physical body being a base externally surrounded by spiritual bodies. Spiritual bodies are essential and high in importance for the developmental step forward, but without the secondary support of a well-functioning physical body, they mean nothing. It's logical that by favoring either the spiritual or the material, we create an imbalance and create a set of serious problems for ourselves. Now I am aware that when I was a spiritual fanatic, I neglected another part of myself. I unintentionally blocked my own access to higher development and remained stuck in one place. The answer is in harmony.

"*He who lives in harmony with himself lives in harmony with the universe.*" -Marcus Aurelius

Day Five of My New Era

I'm no longer waiting for a miracle or the help of someone or something else. Everything is up to me now. I continue to care for myself with great intensity through bioenergy received from healthy and simple foods, I seek nature, I avoid negative thoughts, as well as people and places that cause me harm. I exercise to open all important energy receivers of my body. I strive to remove bad habits from each of my thoughts and actions. To walk through the middle path and stay away from extremes is not as easy as it seems. Balancing opposites, such as selfishness versus selfless service to others that causes harm to self, is much more difficult in everyday life than self-help books lead us to believe.

"*It is only with the heart that one can see rightly; what is essential is invisible to the eye.*" -Antonie de Saint-Exupery

Day Nine of My New Era

I try to do everything as best as I can, without shortcuts or excuses. It is clear that I can only achieve real results with a positive attitude. I continue to learn to calm my mind, the only sure way to eliminate unwanted negative thoughts. It is difficult to keep the mind clean, without constant intrusions and harassment from new thoughts that infiltrate my mind one after another. All of us have this mess of thoughts shouting one over another inside our heads, and this chaos can keep us unnecessarily pre-occupied. I'm learning to ignore it, refuse to deal with it, and just wait for the thoughts to freely vanish on their own. For the more persistent ones, I have to say to myself: "Enough. Leave, out!" It is a necessity and a pre-requisite for the resulting spiritual progress.

A thought has a very significant influence over our emotions. It can dramatically change them and attract life events that are tuned to a similar frequency. My friend Olivia was a perfectly healthy woman. She was very interested in human health and began attending courses about it. She became a hypochondriac. Her mind was constantly occupied with thoughts of what could and couldn't harm her, what every little pain meant, and what bacteria awaited her around every corner. Later, these fantastical scenarios evolved into feelings of illness, only to end up as actual illnesses. The preoccupation in her mind eventually attracted these issues into her life.

"*Those who cannot change their mind cannot do anything.*"

-George Bernard Shaw

Day Twelve of My New Era

After hours of training, I can feel changes within my calm mind. While observing the bright blue sky on the beach, I could see small sparks of silver energy appear and disappear, shine and move around like specks of stardust, see blurred gray clouds of energy dancing around trees like transparent smoke.

I received answers to some of the questions I've been carrying with me all my life. A few times already I've arrived at a clear piece of information and figured out a solution without allowing thoughts to battle within my mind. I believe this non-complicated, non-contemplative approach to problems is called intuition.

It feels good to have this ability to look beneath the spiritual curtain, thanks to my wholesome approach to life. I can determine with more and more accuracy what is true, what is untrue, what is superficial and what is dark energy dressed up in white. I know what to do and when to do it, but my knowledge does not come from reason. It is sudden, clear, pristine, and mine. I am never dependent on getting the answer from somewhere else.

"*Everything has its beauty but not everyone sees it.*" -Confucius

Day Sixteen of My New Era

All available information from scientific or energetically clean sources describes a number of spiritual bodies that surround the physical body of a human.

The closest one, the ethereal body, is compared to the blueprint of our physical form. If the two aren't harmonious, bad things happen. I felt this during a difficult time in my life, when I lived in fear. The emotion extended from the ethereal body into my physical one, and I suffered from digestive tract disorders. After I resolved my fears, I became healthy again. The second body is emotional, responsible for our feelings, and the third, mental, has to do with reason.

Albert Einstein described the physical body as a mass of concentrated energy, heavy, dark, and nearly immobile. Everything is energy, nothing but energy exists, energy that cannot be lost, only transformed. All of us consist of energy and after we die, we simply change form, and according to the law of conservation of energy, we still exist. Energy is not only a matter of physics – we can also talk about the energy of words, thoughts and actions. Scientists claim that everything that vibrates is energy; according to metaphysics, it is a ghost; and believers call it God. Each body that is distant from the physical one is more transparent, lighter, more esoteric and harder to observe. Strong bonds exist between each of the spiritual bodies, and the same bonds also connect them to the physical body. As stated by hermeticism: "Everything is related to everything else, as are links in a fishnet. The top is the bottom, the bottom is the top. Big is small. Inside is outside."

Day Twenty of My New Era

Today, I wasn't able to control a dark thought while dealing with an aggressive person, and like

a boomerang, a textbook example of a reaction immediately hit me back. I was given a sixty dollar ticket for bad parking. Energy grows with whatever we focus on. When I think and act positively, I am successful and good things happen. When I think bad thoughts, I attract negatives. One type of energy attracts more of the same type and enforces it. Opposites repel each other. We can only attract what responds to our vibrations.

Even flowers follow this law of affirmative resonance. Scientists conducted experiments in which they played music and spoke calmly to selected vegetation. The flowers that were thusly pampered grew bigger, healthier and stronger than the others. The law of resonance is the law of energy flow. Every vibration carries inside energy and spreads it onto everything with similar vibrations. What more, energies are synergistic, meaning that the combined power of two beings is bigger than the sum of both when they are measured separately and added only in theory.

"*Misery loves company.*" -Common proverb

Day Twenty-Five of My New Era

I try to do my best in all of my pursuits. There are circumstances I cannot change, and so I adjust my approach instead. Everything really depends on my point of view on situations and people. I can see the glass as half full or half empty. I'm either afraid of the dark tunnel or I look ahead to see the light at its end. I shape the future with my thoughts. Positive thinking can lead to miracles and one of its basic ingredients is laughter, rather effective medicine.

I stopped criticizing, judging, and competing with others. I do my best to understand, to forgive, to avoid manipulating and doing any sort of harm to other people. I cut ties with negative individuals, and my transformed energy no longer attracts the complainers and the eternally entitled. As a matter of fact, I only meet amazing new friends who have positive, interesting things to say. I finally found happiness in love. I consciously made changes in my life every day, and these changes likely brought on this very important phone call. A phone call from HIM!

For the first time in my life, the significant other does not fight with me, does not try to control me, does not try to push me in a direction I don't want to go. Our love is unconditional. We work together, we help each other, and we focus on our victories. This is because HE understands my spiritual background, his energy vibrates on a higher frequency, and he sends out waves of pure goodness that come right back to him. I'm experiencing one of the most beautiful times in my life, and I know it isn't coincidence, but a natural part of the changes I'm undergoing.

"*Gravity is not responsible for people falling in love.*"
-Albert Einstein

Day Twenty-Nine of My New Era

My sensory perception was broadened after I removed roadblocks, cleaned out my mind, fed my physical body healthily and thus enabled it to transmit and receive energy. I subdued the constant buzzing inside my head. For this kind of thought cleansing, it is good to slow down for a few minutes and focus on counting: "First thought, second thought, third thought…"

A moment ago, I returned from a walk on the beach, where I could see a whole new world thanks to my changed perception. When in nature, I can feel myself blend into my surroundings and feel I am a part of the scenery. Sometimes I can spot an image or a flash of light in my peripheral vision; other times I hear a voice or receive information that does not at first seem important, only to realize later it is crucial. I'm learning to understand everything around me and pay attention to every message I'm supposed to hear. Because I'm still learning to walk on this path to extended perception, I sometimes feel nervous for no reason, uncomfortable, sick, and emotionally unstable. I cannot skip this part of the process because everything has its purpose and nothing happens by accident. Every person can learn this, and by doing so help themselves and aid the progress of the entire human race.

"*When all the world is telling you 'no', tell yourself 'yes' ten times louder.*" -Unknown

Day Thirty of My New Era

Today I have so much energy I could hand it out on the street. I met beautiful people who shine with positivity. I don't know how to describe the warmth some people can surround their bodies with by simply being alive. Their existence caresses and embraces at the same time. Though I don't know most of them, they still make me feel incredible. For one, they are clearly people on spiritual rise, and my energy resonates with theirs, encouraging mutual sympathy. I'm sure you know what the opposite feels like, when you speak to a stranger who'd never done any harm to you, but your different energies still clash and you cannot wait for the conversation to be over. It means you're not vibrating on the same wavelength. My ex-partner did not subscribe to a very healthy lifestyle, leaving his body blocked to natural intake of energy. He became addicted to my energy and began stealing it away. Later on, I read up on energy vampires and their harmful effects. After he arrived home, he started feeling great while I grew more and more tired in his presence. If one of the partners becomes a parasite, feeding off of the other's energy, and fails to understand their spiritual basis, it is necessary to leave them behind.

"*Reality is merely an illusion, albeit a very persistent one.*"

-Albert Einstein

Day Thirty-Six of My New Era

A moment ago, I was thinking about my friend, and then she called. I'm sure you know the feeling, intuition telling you to take a different route to work or predicting future events.

Even scientists study these occurrences. Modern science admits the existence of energy, bioenergy, energy fields, and looks at it as life and universe unified in mutual interaction. The theory of relativity is not currently a part of everyday life, but we are familiar with its projections. Let's take time as an example. Sometimes, it runs by quickly, while other times it drags insufferably. When we were children, a week felt like infinity, but as adults, we see it as a fairly short period of time.

I remember an interesting story my friend told me, one that took place when he was a student. One morning, David, his sister, and two other friends traveled to a nearby village to watch a soccer match. About one kilometer before their destination, they drove the car onto a side road leading to the soccer field. Darkness surrounded them and remained until they arrived to the field. Their watches announced five o'clock. The match had ended hours ago and all that remained on the field was the cleaning crew. None of them recalled anything strange happening during the drive, but they were not able to explain the nine hours missing from their lives. David is very interested in this type of unexplained occurrences and believes that their move through time has something to do with energy fields. According to Einstein's theory, waves are present inside the energy fields and cause energy can change and collide. It never merges, but rather cooperates. That is why Dave and his friends could maneuver in time and move into a different energy concentration or dimension, where time flows differently because it can move faster due to smaller resistance.

The same applies to your bioenergy when you find yourself next to an angry individual. His energy field interrupts yours, they begin to resonate, and you feel uncomfortable. I left the angry people behind.

"*Not everything that can be counted counts, and not everything that counts can be counted.*" -Albert Einstein

Day Forty-Four of My New Era

I have an answer to another question. It was published in a geographic magazine. Facts and findings about morphological fields have been published since 1964. Simply put, it is a theory stating that whatever happens in one part of an energy field affects all other parts, too. Immediately.

In 1921, delivery of milk was common in England and many other parts of the world. Every morning, a glass bottle with milk was delivered and placed right on your doorstep. One day, in the town of Southampton, a chickadee bird peeled off the foil bottle cover and drank the milk. Milk deliveries stopped completely during WWII because the bottle-opening and milk-drinking habit of chickadees spread through England and the rest of Europe in no time. The hundredth monkey phenomenon presents a similar case. For thirty years, scientists have been observing Japanese monkey specimens, Macaca fuscata, in their natural environment. These monkeys love to eat potatoes. In year 1952, a female monkey discovered that filthy potatoes can be washed in the creek. She passed this discovery on to her mother and other females of her generation, who then taught their mothers to do the same. During a six year period, all of the young monkeys and portion of the old ones learned to clean muddy potatoes. Let's say that 99 monkeys living on the same island washed potatoes as a hundredth one finally learned how to do it, too. That day, something extraordinary happened. It's as if the hundredth monkey provided the last needed bit of energy to force a breakthrough. The habit immediately spread throughout the entire group and every island and mainland, until all Macaca fuscata monkeys washed potatoes before eating them. One member of the species learned something new and repeated it until the imprint of this information spread inside the energy field of a large group or specimen that has its own specific energy – what we call the morphological field. The mechanism of spreading the potato washing habit amongst monkeys can also be applied to the spread of higher consciousness amongst humans. If a critical amount of people reach higher consciousness, the knowledge will reach the rest of the population automatically, and mankind will finally reach its spiritual evolution. James Redfield describes this process in a very compelling way in his book "Celestine Prophecy."

"*We are what we repeatedly do. Excellence, then, is not an act, but a habit.*" –Aristotle

Day Forty-Six of My New Era

Every person has their own morphological field. It is an integrated, unconscious memory given to every living being. Thanks to bioenergy and the law of attraction, two similar fields react together. They resonate with what I possess. Again we can apply the example of a returning boomerang. When I throw a rock upwards, a feather will not land back on my head. I will receive a concussion from the falling rock. The only thing I won't know is how long it's going to take. If I spend time around begrudging people, it is probably because I resonate with them despite my wishes not to. If the opposite is the case, it's necessary to leave those people behind.

These days, I'm no longer afraid of curses. On their own, curses are bursts of strong energy with a highly concentrated emotional punch, and they can have catastrophic effects. Their carrier is elemental energy that attracts the worshippers of elements, either materialistic skeptics or spiritually abstract theorists. In contrast, a spiritually and materially balanced person is connected to nature and functions as a carrier of bioenergy. Nature's energy is different than magical energy, the source of curses; thus, these two energies don't resonate. Bioenergy will interrupt a curse without any effort needed from the human carrier.

"*Love attracts love.*" -Terezie from Lisieux

Day Fifty of My New Era

Why am I so sure about all of this? It's simple. When I used artificial props, substitutes, and systems, and abused their elemental energy to show me what is right and what I should do, I relied entirely on the answers I received from them. I couldn't assess their accuracy, and so I had to blindly believe in their magic. Proponents of magic masterfully use this tool of blind faith to achieve their goals.

Today, I receive information on my own. Through intuition, thoughts, extraordinary circumstances we inaccurately call coincidences, feelings. They come to me when they're supposed to, when I naturally reach the state of readiness for a particular situation. I can't skip ahead, there are no shortcuts. By the way, I know a person who, all in good faith, set on a spiritual path, gave all of his possessions to the Salvation Army, and began practicing spiritualism without covering his basic material needs. Today, he is a homeless man and roams the streets while talking to surrounding entities no one else but he sees. He jumped ahead to a place he wasn't prepared for, received information that was too advanced for him, and underestimated the necessary material foundation we all need to survive, whether we like it or not.

Two things are important to me: lack of fear and possession of complete certainty. I don't use spells or magic, I don't visualize, I don't make demands, I only foster positive supply of bioenergy into my body and maintain a level of health allowing me to easily absorb the natural flow and expand my consciousness. Thanks to this perfect balance, I always know what to do at the right time, what is important, what is the truth and what is a lie. Many events labeled as miracles are merely an accumulation of positivity resonating with similar flows of energy.

"*The price of anything is the amount of life you exchange for it.*"
-Henry David Thoreau

Day Fifty-Three of My New Era

The dictionary reveals: "In Sanskrit, chakra translates into 'wheel' or 'disc'." chakra marks the place through which energy flows in and out of our body. They are passageways in form of spinning funnels. The more accessible our chakras are, the healthier we become. When our chakras are blocked for an extended period of time, we suffer from illness, depression, and a skewed perception of reality. With the help of a pendulum, I learned to recognize which chakra is open and spinning clockwise as it is supposed to, and which spins in the wrong direction or even closes up.

Energy passing through chakras pulses on a specific frequency, depending on the spiritual advancement of each person. Stronger the vibration, higher the level of spiritual wisdom. Food plays a very important role in this. If my mother once again consumed only heat-prepared food, her vibrations would slow down and the passageway for energy would grow smaller. She would fail to perceive gentle nuances from nature and once again encounter a downfall, illness. Raw food means food that is alive, a carrier of health and electromagnetic energy, a unit scientists have titled Angstroem, or A. Fresh fruits and vegetables vibrate on frequencies between 8,000A and 10,000A, while cooked beef shows the value of 0A.

I remember that my daughters loved to cuddle and remain close to me at all times until the age of two. At that age, children still haven't developed strong chakras, and thus remain in the presence of their mother or father. Because they don't have their own protection in form of energy layers, they can be easily affected by damaging entities. This is why my grandmother always told me not to take my small children to graveyards, old buildings, or sites of tragedies and violent acts, in case they are occupied by negative and evil astral beings. Children can also sense perfectly the condition of their parents' relationship thanks to their respective individual fields.

"*Very little is needed to make a happy life; it is all within yourself, in your way of thinking.*" -Marcus Aurelius

Day Fifty-Eight of My New Era

It's a perfect day. I enjoy my morning jog on the beach and my usual Sunday walk through the Californian farmer's market, a place filled with lovely scents. I feel alive and see the shining energy surrounding fresh fruits and vegetables that I like to purchase here. Naturally, I can't resist the organic honey and smell of lavender flowers and clean herb oil extracts packaged in beautiful glass bottles in style of the French Provence. My boyfriend loves the scent of essential oils, which he pours into our diffusers at home, creating an amazing atmosphere. Daily, we practice special exercises to open our chakras inside a room filled with these scents, an essential routine for those craving spiritual advancement. Individual exercises are wonderfully described and explained in the book "Hands of Light" by Barbara Ann Brennan. We agreed to abandon the world of yoga and my boyfriend no longer practices judo or any other martial arts, as they are connected to unclean energies of history, abuse, symbolism and violence. If we don't ensure our energy centers remain open, all other effort is wasted, like carrying water in a bucket with holes. I could close my chakras by drinking alcohol, feeling envy, treating others poorly, eating processed food, and by neglecting the needs of my physical body. Keeping the body in good shape is the condition for keeping the spiritual bodies active and reaching the point of human evolution. Holistic approach and balance is the key to discovering our hidden inner abilities and using them properly.

"*The truest good is living by nature.*" -Marcus Tullius Cicero

Day Sixty-Two of My New Era

Today, I was a witness to an embarrassing scene played by a middle-aged man at the bank. He was so verbally aggressive that no one was able to explain anything to him. I felt sorry for the bank employees who wanted to help him, but instead had to listen to his insults. This man has closed chakras and the energy flow carrying information to him crashes into closed doors, creating a skewed image of reality and deformed projections of the world. He closes his eyes and ears to incoming information, and does everything he can to aggressively and uncompromisingly convince others of his reality. If this man doesn't change his approach, he will block the supply of all bioenergy and cause a collapse in some part of his body. Absence of energy is the cause of many illnesses, such as sudden organ failure. He can reverse this by practicing relaxation, rest, changing his lifestyle, opening himself to nature, eating raw alkalizing foods, practicing exercises to open and reinforce chakras, and thinking and acting positively.

I don't need to visit the bank to get this kind of experience because I know many people with blocked chakras. I can tell who they are because they cannot handle the present, choosing instead to live in the past or future. They lie, pretend, don't like changes, wait instead of finding immediate solutions, run from responsibility, are unable to say sorry, don't take care of themselves and fail to react to warning signs put out by the body. I do my best to stay in a good physical and spiritual shape to keep my chakras open, but that wasn't always the case in my life. I made mistakes, didn't know the things I write about today. But what matters is not only the information I gathered from other sources, but the real experience I went through myself. I began to understand the many simple rules of creating healthy relationships with others, mechanisms of serious illnesses, and reasons for certain life events and trials. I'm sure of this not because someone told me, but because I can see it function in my own life. With the flow of energy, I feel like a part of nature and as such, I receive flashes of wisdom and knowledge naturally and without any particular spin. Magic could never give me such certainty – it does not possess it. We cannot live with magic, only survive, and we pay a high price for it at the end of our life.

"*Biggest aggression arises between closest species.*"
-Charles Darwin

Day Sixty-Five of My New Era

If I stray from my new path even for a moment, I begin to feel uncomfortable. I recognize the co-dependence between my physical body and spirit with greater intensity as time goes on. Any mistakes in my thoughts, acts and diet lead to the closing of chakras and cutting off passages for needed energy. It is a good warning system, allowing me to immediately make adjustments and avoid illnesses and mistakes in important life decisions. I know exactly what happened when I browse the list of my past health issues. Usually, I find the cause in the area of spirituality, my former judgments about the world. Today, I spoke to a friend who is very open to these issues. She asked a question that all of us likely think of at some point, one I used to ask myself: "It's so simple, it's suspicious." Yes. That's how mistaken we humans are.

"*Life is really very simple, and we only complicate it by insisting on its complexity.*" -Confucius

Day Sixty-Nine of My New Era

Like every other person, I entered this world spiritually unaware and equipped only with logic, emotions and will, all of which are connected together by a consciousness that is, as I mentioned, blind to the spiritual. To simplify; every person not awake does not possess balanced emotions, logic and will, these three parts make up the human consciousness. But when we manage to harmonize, we wake up and climb the spiritual ladder of evolution. As I child, I was led to materialism. "If you can touch it, it matters. Everything else is nonsense. Go where everybody else is going, it's the right direction. Listen to experts and leaders, they are always right…" That's what they taught me at home, in school and on television, and I believed them. My spirituality leaned toward one side, causing me to be spiritually ignorant. My father did not help this situation. As a typical materialist, he calculates everything in the context of chickens. He loves eating chicken so much that it became his way of measuring value. When my mother bough a brand new set of China plates, my father immediately estimated it was worth at least twenty cooked chickens. When I told him about my new car, he asked: "How many chickens did it cost?" Had I not attended school, I would now be counting in chickens. Anything that could not be calculated into chicken units was at my house considered worthless. To talk about balance in these conditions would have been, naturally, taken as a joke.

While in university, I took a test in religious studies, a field that examines the beginnings and development of religious thinking and religion in general. It was a mandatory test for all students of humanities at my university and did not attract any special attention. For me, however, it allowed a deeper look into spiritual spheres and unleashed thousands of questions. That's when I started digging through books and other sources of information. I crossed over to the other extreme, feeding my soul but ignoring the rest. There was no balance; I was overwhelmed by the emotional sphere. Though I was finally paying attention to the spiritual, I became ignorant in a different way. My will, as always, adjusted itself to my current preferences and made the imbalance even worse. I didn't know that back then, I couldn't recognize the correct path. I believed that spiritual teachers, books, tarot cards and other tools already held all the information available. I could only follow, cast spells, repeat hours of mantras, and continue to be dependent on someone or something to find answers. There was a constant submission of someone to something. If you use this candle and repeat a request to the powers of fire ten times, your wish will be fulfilled. If you repeat a certain mantra according to the instructions of a guru and touch Indian praying marbles, you will free your spirit and achieve the state of nirvana during your meditations. We were not born to always set conditions upon everything, to struggle with chaos and uncertainty, but to prosper in harmony. How we act translates into what happens to us. We get what we deserve. If we twist something, it will come back to haunt us.

"*Happiness is not being pained in body or troubled in mind.*"

-Thomas Jefferson

Day Seventy of My New Era

Raw food, exercise, open chakras, discarded artificial practices, elimination of negative energy around me, daily routine improvement of my person, and contact with nature set my intellect, emotions and will into an equilibrium and I shone the light into a dark corner. My consciousness expanded, and I achieved a state of harmony and stability with access to bioenergy, a carrier of information from nature. Through intuition, signs, encounters with people and their prophecies, visions, and clear feelings, I receive unmodified truths and instructions from nature and the universe. Bioenergy flows through me on its own, I don't need to ask or summon it. It resonates with me when I am tuned to its frequency. Only I can tune myself, there is no interference from another place. When my harmony falters, it tips to one side and causes decrease in energy. That is when I have to return to the basics, a harmonic arranging of logic, emotions and will through my daily personal improvement.

Some people with permanently extended consciousness can even heal the sick. They do not heal in the usual sense of the word; rather, they are well-tuned to the open flows of energy in nature and serve the sick as a channel through which the healing bioenergy can make its way. The rise and fall of bioenergetics frequency can also determine the quality of a person's life. An uncle of mine has lived since childhood in an isolated house in the European mountains. He does not read or study, but he is so well-tuned he receives bioenergy from nature to fuel his healthy common sense. He isn't the smartest person on the planet, but he is certainly one of the wisest.

"*The invariable work of wisdom is to see the miraculous in the common.*" -Ralph Waldo Emerson

Day Seventy-Three of My New Era

Thanks to my strength of will, I can perceive details I couldn't have noticed when I was plagued with my past disharmonies. More and more often I can count on my feelings and intuition. I can naturally accept people for who they are. I don't manipulate them or my own self. I treat others with love and without conditions. I can tune into human motives and emotions with ease and grace. I can objectively judge why a person acted in a certain way without involving my personal opinions and value systems. I show respect. This outlook on others and myself wasn't always so automatic for me. Today, I see myself from within, with the eyes of a whole and individual self at the same time. There are no coincidences, no encounter is without a purpose, and every person tells me things that can have a significant impact in future, even if it doesn't seem like it at first. I learned to understand prophecies. Even unpleasant situations or experiences exist to teach me something, and I am grateful for them. My awoken sensors recognize and signalize reliably truth and lies. Reason used to exclusively perform that task, but now it only passively looks on. In the past, I flew in low altitudes, surrounded by fog of deception and manipulation. My newly gained harmony increased the inner frequency of bioenergy and carried me high above the fog and clouds. Everything is clear, perfectly visible. I observe life from above, in contours of truth, without curtains, masks and haze. I can even see the creators of this fog right above the ground. They are very busy. They cover certain places with layers of fog to twist the truth. The lower the visibility, the higher chance for manipulation and growth of business. It isn't true that all paths lead to one destination – it's only something spiritual leaders say to those lost and desperate to believe. I only see one path leading to human evolution. It is filled with healthy, vital people, those who responsibly care for their own health and shine with the energy of nature's creative strength. On its end is not the destruction all previous civilizations had reached under the influence of magic, but an impressively bright future.

"*Man is the measure of all things.*" -Protagoras

Day Seventy-Six of My New Era

I only receive information tuned to my inner self, the kind that resonates. Moments of absolute silence, privacy without any noise, television, radio, cell phone, computers or people are absolutely necessary. The need for peace, my own time, calmness, and avoidance of loud sounds comes along with the spiritual rise. I train myself to quickly disconnect from reality during moments that require all of my attention to catch a piece of information I'm supposed to receive. Without it, I could make the wrong decision and choose a wrong path or take a shortcut, missing a purpose I was supposed to fulfill in this life. First thought, second though, third thought…

"*Every day is a small life, every awakening is a small birth, every morning is a small youth and every night is a small death.*"
-Arthur Shopenauer

Day Eighty of My New Era

If I continue to increase my inner bioenergy frequency, I have a chance to achieve the state of knowing perfection and absolute truth. People who routinely experience this speak of a flash, discovery of the possibility of becoming one with the universe, a mystical experience. During prolonged exposures to inner balance, the merging of the soul and spirit, understanding reincarnation, obtaining info from previous lives and understanding their current purpose, they begin to talk about the spiritual level of enlightenment. These people experience visions, their intuition becomes impeccably precise, and they can read nature and the universe and understand its strengths and weaknesses.

Any person, me included, can reach this state of being if we discard the old, ineffective methods. Magic, religion, or any other force cannot lead humans forward because they had already failed us throughout history. We must all begin with our own respective self. If we can achieve the needed balance, we can rise spiritually and take active control over our lives. Nature and our planet will heal and the negative forces leading humanity to its destruction will not resonate with anyone or anything, and eventually cease to exist.

"*Nature does nothing without purpose or uselessly.*" -Aristotle

Day Eighty-Five of My New Era

My previous artificial spiritual orientation outlined karma as a memory of past actions that I'll be sooner or later punished for. Today I know that difficult life situations are not payback, but collected energy of all previous poorly handled situations that suddenly re-appear, like pieces of trash I kicked underneath the living room couch. Will I handle this repeated situation and manage to clean the mess, or will I decide to be filthy again and contribute more garbage to the mounting pile?

When I want to reach higher spiritual grounds with clean form, without magic, I need to change, and that's when karma comes in handy. Karma is not a prison guard, but a teacher educating me, you, every living being. If I can resolve all of my affairs in this life without mistakes, I'll eliminate all leftovers of negative energy and find my life clean of tragedies, cruel strikes of fate, and unpleasant situations. Karma gets us into a situation similar to those in the past, testing whether we have learned from the previous missteps and can make the right decisions this time around. If we pass, we remove the garbage cluttering our personal landfill and eliminate a whole karmic layer.

Throughout my life, I was unsuccessful in romantic relationships. After painful events that repeated themselves in different scenarios, I learned what I did wrong and why I chose the same partners over and over again. I learned my lesson and met the man with whom I have an amazing, harmonious relationship.

"*Let him that would move the world first move himself.*"

-Socrates

Day Eighty-Eight of My New Era

Though I'm undergoing a karmic cleansing that can last for months or years and don't always feel without fault, I'm aware of my luck in finding this path. Because I daily cleanse my chakras through exercise, eat alkalizing, plant-based and raw foods, avoid negative people, places and situations, and do my best to spend time in nature daily, or at least hug a tree, my spiritual development rises. Those who want to walk this path must get rid of bad habits, such as smoking, drinking even small amounts of alcohol, the habit of bad-mouthing and judging...you know which ones apply to you. As long as I'm on the rise, I can be certain that I won't face difficult life situations, those intruding into our lives when we insist on being dedicated materialists or mistakenly believe we are on the right spiritual path. In those cases, karma cleansing can also be achieved. The cleansing happens suddenly, unforeseeably, and often dramatically. Before making its appearance, karma festers, like expired canned pickles resting in stinking juice. The longer these pickles stay in the glass, the louder explosion will follow the opening of the jar. Our mistakes and missteps pile up in a similar way, until our body cannot handle any more contamination and needs to cleanse itself. We gather life errors, bad decisions, small and big ethical violations, anger, negativity, selfishness, harming others…The self-induced karmic cleansing then brings energy that causes serious illness, accidents, divorce, bad luck, catastrophes, and we are forced to face situations that come around because our karma hasn't been cleansed before, or wasn't cleansed enough. We are supposed to show if and how we can deal with difficult situations and whether we've learned enough since to avoid making the same mistakes. If we make the wrong choices again, a new layer of negative karma will form, and similar events will repeat again and again.

Logically, I do what I can to remain in balance and thus pass through the gentler path of karmic cleansing. We all have karma and its cleansing occurs without exceptions. It doesn't matter if we believe in karma or deny it. I keep this peeling of rotted layers firmly under my own direction. Instead of waiting, I take active part in my own life. By getting rid of old karma layers systematically, I can avoid unexpected life situations and ease my path to the next evolutionary step of becoming a human firmly connected to nature, its infinite wisdom flowing through my veins all the way to enlightenment. Everyone can reach this point on their own, with the right amount of dedication and involvement.

"If a person is unhappy with their lifestyle, they can change it in two ways. Either change the life conditions, or spiritual stance. The first is not always possible, but the second is."
-Ralph Waldo Emerson

Day Ninety-Two of My New Era

I feel my life is calmer and I'm no longer dragged around by circumstances. It's thanks to the harmonic balancing I work on every day. I experience small downswings, mostly likely because of the rotten juice spilling out of the jar. It could be worse – I could be stuck in ignorance and remain in the stinking pickle jar forever. I left behind the script of: "Drama in my life and repeated impossible situations." I control the causes, and thus all the effects that follow are expected and acceptable.

"*He who loves practice without theory is like the sailor who boards ship without a rudder and compass and never knows where he may cast.*" -Leonardo da Vinci

Day Ninety-Five of My New Era

Lately, I am not very sociable, but today is an exception. A friend of mine is celebrating her birthday and her garden is full of guests, beautiful people inside and out. Anna is surrounded by an incredible family, beautiful and healthy children, she is practically drowning in money, and she built a fantastic career and marriage. Her life is happy and harmonious, she doesn't need to worry about unsolvable problems, she doesn't face any tragedies, and her life flows through a crystal clear current. My friend is the perfect example of a person with clean karma. She knows how to laugh and share her love and peace, and this sharing resonates with the additional flows of positive energy attached to her. One day in her company feels like a month-long stay in a luxurious spa.

"*We become what we think about all day long.*"
-Ralph Waldo Emerson

Day Ninety-Seven of My New Era

My time with intellectual magic, a time that has fortunately passed, also affected my karma. Most spiritual schools of thoughts mistakenly claim that we should be happy, that negative situations follow you, embrace them. If you can take the punishment, some higher force will forgive a past mistake or bad deed.

These methods of regression, deep therapy and others are really just a way of picking through the garbage of karmic layers. That's why there is a danger of passing into another state of consciousness or unexpected opening of karmic history that will then repeat itself. Usually, a tragedy follows, an unexpected, drastic version of settling an old debt. One cannot predict how old the debt will be, time has no place here. What more, the uncovered negative energy of karma attracts the same energy back into the person's life. Magic has the ability to postpone the effects of karma, but it cannot cleanse it. That is why a person's karma can collect with such force, until the individual is plagued with serious illness threatening their life.

In a similar way, the layers of karma gathered by our planet over time initiated self-cleaning in form of natural disasters. Harmony of matter, body and soul is the only path to increase the frequency of bioenergy. Returning to nature is the only path to evolution. I'm at the beginning and I can already feel big changes and real progress. Karma is not a prison guard, but an educator. When I'm tuned correctly, I receive automatic signals whenever I make a mistake, and I correct it right away. Balance and harmony ensure I don't miss the signal. It is too bad that so often people hear but don't listen, see but oversee, and let themselves be led on a leash, blind and careless.

"*Nothing can be created out of nothing.*" -Lucretius

Day Ninety-Nine of My New Era

I know with certainty that whatever I don't achieve on my own in life, I won't have. I have this one life, shaped like a big stage, this one body like a theater building, one hosting the performances that take place during my lifetime. Every detail is saved to a hard drive, one that includes all information, situations, dialogues, monologues and actions as memories of my current existence on this Earth. After I die, I'll leave the theater building and my astral spiritual body will take a break from performing. As soon as I receive a new gig at another theater, I'll use the same hard drive and record a new file, new life in another body, with some characters and situations being similar to the previous ones. All of this repeats until I learn everything I'm supposed to understand and resolve all relationships and problems. Though my memory of the previous life is concealed, sometimes it makes an appearance in form of déjà vu or fragments of memories. We can only advance through evolution here, inside our physical bodies. Only here and now we can cleanse ourselves and become better beings. Recording and erasing material from the hard drive only happens because of the body and its movement through matter, here on Earth.

"*Skepticism is a slow suicide.*" -Ralph Waldo Emerson

Day Hundred and One of My New Era

I reap what I sow. That is the common definition of karma. If you harm someone, sooner or later you'll be harmed in a similar way. If you save someone's life, you may be rewarded with an unexpected financial infusion that will save you. We are talking about the law of cause and effect. If someone's fate takes a turn and they are suddenly unsuccessful, unlucky, it means they've collected past energies of wrong acts that haven't been processed correctly. Karma is the mirror to our past. The mirror shows a perfect reflection of previous actions, without any deformations. What happens to me is not caused by karma, it's all me. This means that everything I do is a seed from which my tomorrow will grow.

If I throw a stone at someone and harm then, they will throw a rock at someone else and so on. Let's say that stone number thirty-three hits me again. It breaks my skull and kills me. This is also how karma works. I took a major part in the situation because I started it. Others got involved, but only partially. At the beginning, I put the highest amount of negative and destructive energy into the act, and the energy came back to me in equal force. When I commit a wrong act, I must realize it immediately, apologize and make up for it. A quick apology can sometimes be miraculously effective. If I leave it be, the consequences of my act will spread like a cloud of poisonous gas and grow until they affect too many human lives, and apology becomes impossible.

Karma is just. It cannot be corrupted or tricked. A person can choose the first path and live through difficult circumstances, tragedies and illnesses, and undergo many tests that have to do with karmic cleansing. Or, they can choose to spiritually awaken and balance the spiritual and material by maintaining a perfect diet, opening chakras, spending time in nature and eliminating influence of bad acts and people in their life.

"*Every new beginning comes from some other beginning's end.*"
-Lucius Seneca

Day One Hundred and Two of My New Era

I managed to master the study of a fine art: silence. I didn't realize just how much I used to talk without any particular purpose. Not only were my own words often used against me; they held much more power than I anticipated. Eastern cultures are aware of the laws of silence and corresponding energies, and that is why they belong among the most soft-spoken people in the world. They realized that thoughts with deeper charge need to be captured and held.

A Japanese friend of mine explained to me a few months ago that a thought should not be expressed immediately, but rather kept, nurtured by silence, strengthened, until it gains mass and ripens. A properly enforced idea attracts similar forms of thought and thus grows even more. Through such connections we achieve perfection and inspiration. She taught me how to keep away from empty and irrational ideas. This is necessary, because all thoughts come back to a place of departure. She always said: "If you create thoughts, you use a powerful force that can help you reach grounds higher and more pure."

"*Wise men speak because they have something to say; Fools because they have to say something.*" -Plato

Day One Hundred and Three of My New Era

"During their passage into the fifth dimension, small children sometimes help their parents with the journey" or "There will be a possibility of survival on giant space ships or by passing directly into the fifth dimension." These and other pieces of nonsense are offered by current spiritual texts. Most of the time they are shouts in the dark without any deeper understanding or logic which often confuse and disorient readers. Most amateurs have trouble imagining the term "dimension" at all. First dimension can be seen as points A and B, connected by a stem of grass on which a fly crawls in a straight line. A fly moving along the length and width of an empty coconut surface is in the space of two dimensions. When it flies inside the coconut, it finds itself in the space of three dimensions. Fourth dimension adds a quantity of time to the third dimension, making it difficult for us to comprehend.

"*An attempt at visualizing the Fourth Dimension: Take a point, stretch it into a line, curl it into a circle, twist it into a sphere, and punch through the sphere.*" -Albert Einstein

Day One Hundred and Five of My New Era

I read an interesting article today about an event that took place in 1944 Estonia, during WWII. Soviet soldiers encountered a group of cavalry soldiers dressed in old-fashioned uniforms. When the soldiers on horseback spotted the tanks and new weapon technology, they fled. The Soviets managed to take one captive, but he only spoke French and claimed he was a member of Napoleon's army. He said his brigade got lost in a thick fog and was looking for a way back. When asked when he was born, the soldier answered with year 1772. A similar story took place in the 80s, when a Russian submarine appeared in the middle of the Pacific Ocean and was ordered to emerge. The submarine crew members were surprised to find Japanese WWII ship floating right above them. On board, they found a half-dead Japanese sailor whose identification papers dated back to year 1940. These occurrences, along with the widely discussed Philadelphia Experiment, are examples of movement in time and space. During an experiment conducted in 1943, a USS Navy destroyer escort Eldridge was concealed inside a magnetic bottle and, after activation of the magnetic case, became invisible to radars. On top of that, the ship completely disappeared. It materialized again 400 miles away, near Norfolk. Bodies of some of the crew members were, after the change in space-time continuum and following materialization, embedded into the steel ship construction. Those who survived suffered from heavy physical and psychological damage and were again pulled out of our space and time. In this context, there are also rumors of another secret American experiment, titled "Phoenix."

"*Do not grow old, no matter how long you live. Never cease to stand like curious children before the Great Mystery into which we were born.*" -Albert Einstein

Day One Hundred and Nine of My New Era

Many books with spiritual focus cover the topic of dimensions. Most of the time, they claim that while a person grows spiritually, they pass from one dimension to the other. Higher progress equals higher dimension. They consider dimensions to be geometrically layered wrappers following one after another. They pass over the multi-dimensional quantum approach. A religious and spiritual book titled Urantia describes the 12 dimensions in a similar way.

Very popular amongst spiritual teachers and schools is the emphasis on a fifth dimension, the one where all of us are allegedly headed. The basics of their artificial theory consist of elemental energy that's supposed to help us get rid of our physical bodies and escort the soul to the fifth dimensions.

Let's take for example a person in poor health, living a neglected lifestyle, refusing to love themselves, a person that is materially lacking. Our person, however, spends hours daily meditating and repeating special mantras recommended to him by a guru, mantras that will someday get him to a state allowing separation of spirit and body. He smiles all day, gives people love, acts ethically. He is bound to a single area of emotion and lacks the balance with material and physical areas. He only cares about one thing, to spiritually achieve the level of fifth dimension. But without his physical body and the Earth, he cannot advance and improve. His spiritual imprint will, after leaving the body, await another opportunity to gain a body and take another step in its evolution. The only way he can achieve a higher sphere is by staying on Earth and finding the path to spiritual advancement here.

"*Everyone thinks of changing the world, but no one thinks of changing himself.*" -Leo Tolstoy

Day One Hundred and Ten of My New Era

I must achieve harmony here on Earth. Only here reside the visible opposites between which I'm supposed to place an equality sign. Every day I try to find the middle ground between good and evil, beautiful and ugly, caring and selfishness, happiness and sadness, depth and superficiality, matter and spirit. The goal of evolution is to tune all opposing pairs into a balance. Just the fact I can notice each one means I'm attempting to understand a given problem or mistake, learn from it, make up for it and improve as a person. This common balancing is quite fun and also the foundation of human development. This means that if I left this world tipped into the emotional area without tuning myself into a good material life and a healthy body, I would remain unclean. In my next life, I would need to balance the material responsibility I neglected. I'm in no rush to get into the widely publicized astral sphere. Astral is not a destination, only a waiting room, a rest stop between two lives. A place where our recorded history rests before another life begins. That's the only reason we should concern ourselves with the astral sphere. Some people tend of overestimate it, begin to communicate with astral beings and often gain wrong ideas and gather incorrect information.

"*Life belongs to the living and he who lives must be prepared for changes.*" -Johann Wolfgang Goethe

Day One Hundred and Thirteen of My New Era

I think that instead of using the word dimension, we should say level. By that I mean level of cleanliness, truth, spiritual maturity, bioenergy, simply a level on which we are all tuned. Every person has their own.

Logically I can see that levels or dimensions are parallel, passing through each other, but they never mix, staying separated thanks to different density. The first dimension is most dense, material; it can be perceived by our senses and measured by machines. The next level is astral, a place where souls pass through a tunnel after the physical death of every human, even those who don't believe in it. The Dark Dimension is filled with manipulative energies and heavily clogged karmic layers. At last, the Light Dimension is created with the positive bioenergy of nature, our planet, the universe and cosmos. This is a fairly explainable conception of the multidimensional space divided by different energies. Unfortunately, it is often wrongly interpreted. A human is considered to be a whole, an indivisible being.

We do not physically rise into a dimension. A dimension is the level of spiritual cleanliness, harmony and maturity of a human. Here, not elsewhere! All dimensions are here, next to us, in front of us, above us, behind us, we are inside of them, all of them at once, they are everywhere, only we do not see or feel them. It's as if we are in one of them, and we can only feel it because we are tuned to it and resonate with it. We attract it with our thoughts, acts and deeds. Those who are spiritually awakened vibrate on a higher frequency, thus sometimes penetrating another dimension.

"*We first make our habits, then our habits make us.*"
-John Dryden

Day One Hundred and Fifteen of My New Era

The developmental ascent is called evolution and it is exactly what awaits us in near future. I'm not talking about alarmist messages announcing the end of the world. But we should certainly anticipate significant natural, political, economic and personal changes. People will be forced to make important life decisions.

Things they try to defend themselves against the most will strike with double the usual force, and who individuals are and what they resonate with will become dominant in their lives. Many already feel it today. It is a process, not a single-strike change. One of the reasons is the necessity of reversal, forced by nature destroyed, exhausted and violated by human presence, a corrupted human society, and a lack of balance in human knowledge.

Another reason will be the changes in positioning of the Earth and Sun within the universe. I've read many scientific texts explaining that our planet will, on its passage through the universe, soon enter a path of different energy created by photons vibrating on a very high frequency. Photon energy will change relationships on Earth not only economically, but even adjust humanity's thought process. Photons will someday be a resource for transportation, industry, a cure to all illnesses and a key to making our spiritual advancement and unlocking of special abilities easier. Photons will supposedly become our new lifestyle.

According to scientists, we enter the photon passage approximately once every 11,000 years, and remain there for 2,000 years. We always encounter a sharp rise or a deep fall. The latest example was the era of Atlantis. More submersions in the photon area had already begun, and twice we needed to adjust the atomic world clock to make up for our passage into the galactic time. It shouldn't be a sudden change, but a slow process that will happen

in waves. I perceive time differently than I used to. It flies more quickly.

"*The secret of change is to focus all of your time energy, not on fighting the old, but building the new.*" -Socrates

Day One Hundred and Sixteen of My New Era

When I split a photograph into four pieces, each piece will have a part of a house and a garden on it. I cut up a 3D hologram photo of a house with a garden. In front of me I have four quarters and each holds an image of the whole house and garden. I see four houses and four gardens in a smaller form. Even if I split them into thousands of pieces, every piece will show me an entire house and a garden. A hologram carries a whole in each part. David Bohm, a physicist from University of London, believed that the essence of the material universe and everything in it is a hologram. According to him, we cannot perceive the deeper levels of reality in the universe because it is hidden from us, we only see a piece, we cannot spot a dimension behind our scope of vision. We are used to studying a whole by dissecting it and studying its individual parts. A hologram cannot be divided into parts, only into smaller wholes; there is not a single point or place divided from another by time or space. Everything is connected to everything else, every piece of information in the human brain is

connected to another and is simultaneously shared by the

brains of all other humans. We are able to consciously create our own lives and as creators, we are connected.

"*I speak to everyone in the same way, weather he is the garbage man or the president of university.*" -Albert Einstein

Day One Hundred and Seventeen of My New Era

I create everything with my senses, nothing happens by accident. Whatever good or bad happened in my life, every event always had its cause and effect. At times I questioned why something terrible happened when I hadn't made any significant mistakes for a while. Time and space have nothing to do with a given moment. Sometimes we must settle a karmic debt immediately, sometimes in the next life, but we can always count on being held accountable. True justice has little to do with earthly concepts of laws, punishments, and the hierarchy of human values

Day One Hundred and Nineteen of the New Era

My car died on the way to Los Angeles from San Diego. That I had to wait for an hour for the towing truck to arrive and then spend more time taking care of formalities is only one possible reality in row of options that were available at that moment. Hugh Everett, an American physicist, claims in his quantum theory that in every moment a number of realities, or alternative worlds, exist at once. We only see the option we choose to focus on, and thus fail to see all of the other options from a palette of parallel worlds. Through my feelings, I attracted a situation of malfunction. This means that there was also a possibility of not traveling or a comfortable, malfunction-free transportation home, but also a chance of a serious accident. According to Everett, multiple versions of a single story take part at once and we subconsciously attract the one we energetically resonate with.

My mother's illness was similar. Scenario number one, healthy lifestyle and no illness, scenario number two illness, but also self-improvement and lifestyle change leading to remission. Scenario number three is unhealthy lifestyle, illness, self-pity, life without changes, and tragic results. There was a tricky obstacle in the way - fear. If she couldn't banish fear from her mind, then the feeling of "I fear cancer" would bring the cancer back. A deep feeling coming from her insides. Not words. Those can only interrupt, but not intervene. Feeling is the only language the universe speaks. It cannot comprehend prayers, mantras, wishes, words, human languages. It only communicates through emotions.

Speech and prayer have their purpose, but they are never the deciding factor. They soothe the mind, help stop the constant flow of thoughts, tune a person to a certain emotion, and that is all. Feeling is the key to the scenario that will be chosen for me in the next moment. What I live through and what I carry inside of me cannot be swindled.

"*The most beautiful thing we can experience is the mysterious; it is the source of all true art and science. He who knows it not and can no longer wonder, no longer feel amazement, is as good as dead, a snuffed-out candle.*" -Albert Einstein

Day One Hundred and Twenty-Two of My New Era

Sometime before the New Era, I asked a guru for help. He gave me a mantra and instructions for how many times I need to repeat it daily and ask for my ex-boyfriend to stop using drugs and destroying our lives. I think that there was too much dependence and emphasis on results which, through the repetition of the word drug, concentrated large amounts of energy into the addiction and strengthened it.

Mother, on the contrary, surrounded herself with health, carrots, cabbage, apples, oranges, laughter, ease, active progress of building, inner feeling of vitality, and refused to allow dark thoughts to settle in her mind. She attracted good health.

"*I dream my painting and I paint my dream.*"
-Vincent Van Gogh

Day One Hundred and Twenty-Three of My New Era

I was very fortunate to almost fanatically consume only raw foods. They brought me natural bioenergy holding valuable information that lit up my mind and let me to the right path. This led to expansion of my consciousness and I obtained a personal indicator of truth. The indicator lets me feel what I should and shouldn't eat, where I should and shouldn't go, intuition tells me what is a good choice and who hides behind a crooked mask. It is quite fun to see and hear through means other than sight and hearing. Thanks to the intelligence of natural energy gained from raw foods, I stopped pursuing exclusively spiritual information and evened myself out on the material level. When I felt my bioenergy frequency decreased, I returned to the basics and balanced my feelings, reason and will. I noticed that the people I know who'd never reached this knowledge and purposely shun the physical make it easier for dark influences to take over our world. Progress will come after the balancing of spiritual and physical spheres. In the old Atlantis, humanity passed completely into the spiritual sphere and magic became the sole source of their truth. The result was a complete devastation of nature, the material parts of life, and eventually the Atlantian civilization. Humans were then thrown to the very bottom of evolutionary development and had to start over. They lived in caves, hunted animals, and learned to make fire. We face the same choice they did. Will we act differently?"

I do not know with what weapons World War III will be fought, but World War IV will be fought with sticks and stones."
-Albert Einstein

Day One Hundred and Twenty-Five of My New Era

I establish increasingly better communication with nature. I receive more frequent impulses and easy-to-understand advice. I am not turned toward my inner self, I don't look there for solutions or help. I'm open to receive energy from the universe. I can open myself up to nature's energy anytime and receive its relief, advice, or bring healing to someone else. When I am tuned to its resonance, its healing energy starts channeling through me.

Magic, on the other hand, will take elemental energy anytime it wants it, isn't certain whether the information it receives is true, and has no idea if the receiving person is ready for it. The trick is in allowing the energy to flow freely. I don't control it, influence it, or abuse it. Free flow. That's all. The wisdom of nature's energy is in its ability to give me only what's good for me, regardless of what I think or wish for. I am grateful to nature for many things.

For example, the wishes I had it never fulfilled, those that I now know were wrong. Thank you.

"*Not walking forward means walking backwards.*"
-Walther von der Vegelweille

Day One Hundred and Twenty-Six of My New Era

According to scientists, we are all a part of one universe, and that universe understands one language, the language of feelings, convictions, anticipation, simply emotions. When quality emotions pass into our energy field, the universe captures the quality and provides us accordingly with a life script.

"*It is easier to fight for principles than to live by them.*"
-Alfred Adler.

Day One Hundred and Twenty-Nine of My New Era

I learn and I understand. I understand why I have been so unhappy in my romantic relationships throughout life. It was not bad luck. It was my own reflection in the mirror. A mirror does not break, it does not malfunction. In it, I saw a large, complicated labyrinth of my own critical flaws. I always fell for the person that was supposed to fill in whatever I was missing. Of course, I didn't see it like that back then. Having some distance, I can see clearly that I looked for wholeness, a missing part of the mosaic, something I wasn't getting. The more complex a person becomes, the more conscientious they become in their search for a partner with whom they can build, not only fill old gaps.

"*A small thing can often pose a mirror to a big thing and expose the truth.*" -Lucretius

Day One Hundred and Thirty-Three of My New Era

My boyfriend feels strongly that he was a Native American in his previous life. He is fascinated by their connection with nature and believes firmly that when a person stops reasoning so much, tunes out the noise and builds good physical form, they will find on their own that Mandala will not bring them to nature. Through inner cleanliness, harmony, spiritual awakening on Earth, in the physical body that is healthily nourished and aware, can a Native American and each one of us live a healthy life of one hundred and twenty years.

One thing is certain. Evolution goes on and it doesn't matter whether you and I like it or not. We all go through it. Some can handle it and follow the path independently and consciously, some are pushed to it by illnesses and personal tragedies, some fall off. Daily I see many people trapped in uncomfortable situations. They cannot handle financial and personal crises and seek help from drugs, medication, alcohol and other escape routes. They become depressed, stressed, and seek drastic action. They send out negative energy, receive the same and wonder why nothing good comes to them. Often they experience a chain reaction of one misfortune after another. Generally speaking, this will always apply: "What is bad will become worse. What is good will become better." The choice is ours. It doesn't belong to the events that happen to us.

Day One Hundred and Thirty-Five of My New Era

Those who pass through the evolutionary filter, the cleansing process of the self, detoxification of the planet, tune physical and spiritual opposites into a balanced state, heal their bodies, and open chakras to receive bioenergy will know exactly what to do, attract good things and, without complications, step into the era of light, where ethics will be the basis for making decisions.

If thousands of people continue to walk in their usual paths and do everything the same way they always had, they will not enter the next level. Progress means that one person does something different, better, and others join in. That is the reason why I don't rely on the opinion of people around me. I started with myself. I discarded the comfortable mask of a victim and created my own life. No effort is wasted; even the smallest particle affects the whole. Wherever it focuses its attention, a similar reality is created.

"*Trifles go to make perfection, And perfection is no trifle.*"

-Michelangelo Buonarotti

Day One Hundred and Thirty-Seven of My New Era

In the last chapter of the book The Celestine Prophecy, titled The Emerging Culture, author James Redfield proposed a vision of the future that will change due to evolution. He anticipates that when a critical number of people reach the borders of advanced consciousness, this state of being will reach the entire human race through morphological fields. We'll reach it through natural desire. The author writes that there will be far more places in nature charged with extraordinarily strong energy, and no one will harm nature. Food, drink, transportation and clothing will be accessible to all automatically and free of charge. Money will play a different and less significant role, stockpiling of material goods and the need to manipulate and control will vanish, much like selfishness and sloth. Intuition will be the precise measure of truth and certainty. Humans will purposely decrease their own population, extend their age and use bioenergy for healing. We will naturally give and receive in return. People will communicate through the exchange of energy. Everything will become clearer, easier, more spiritual thanks to higher vibrations. The human body will cease to be a collection of dense energy and become a thinner structure with the ability to vibrate with a similarly tuned dimension. A person will not leave the body for another dimension, they'll stay here and vibrate on gentler frequencies and thus attract more noble energy. Through this enlightenment, people will attract universal energy that will react to their expectations.

"*Your life is what your thoughts make it.*" -Marcus Aurelius

Day One Hundred and Forty of My New Era

Our brain works like a hologram. The universe is in its essence a hologram, too. If the mathematical root of one percent of Earth's human inhabitants expands their consciousness, there is a big possibility the change will massively occur in the collective minds of seven billion people. Scientific research supports this evolutionary principle. Whenever a change occurs in a hologram, the change is reflected in the entire picture. We are only limited by our faith. Every one of us is capable of changing the planet's hologram.

"*In this life we cannot do great things. We can only do small things with great love.*" -Mother Teresa

Day One Hundred and Forty-Two of My New Era

I hope that the children being born today will learn early how to care for their bodies and souls, and that the laws of the universe will be taught in schools. Hopefully they will know that even money is controlled by the universal law of "natural flow of give and take," which states that the flow must be constant, like a river, and if the flow is interrupted, it will be followed by stagnation and build-up that will through the pressure of its own strength destroy itself. Much like the energy that cannot freely flow within the body and builds up causes illness. The principle of give and take is crucial in nature, too. If we interrupt the give or take, we sabotage the financial system of the future, one that instructs: "do more, you will get more," where personal responsibility is much more important than pointing fingers at others. We must take every second for what it is, and replace the word "problem" with the word "opportunity." The universal law of give and take is based on the conviction that people were not born on this earth to live in need and poverty. The perfect accounting results in "law that gives gave," in its essence another version of cause and effect. The universal "law of detachment" states that wherever attachment exists, there is poverty, and wherever detachment occurs, big riches and creative consciousness follow. Similarly simple and clear is the "law of focus," meaning that wherever our attention goes, energy follows. Among them is service to humanity.

I saw this in my friend Jan. He entered small business ventures a few times, but he was always afraid, depressed and worried that things would not work out. He wanted to succeed, but his inner focus was on fear and failure. The more money he made, the more he saved. He held his wealth, took and never gave anyone a cent. Whenever he encountered any issues, he never blamed himself, only others, and he considered every problem to be life-ending and a reason for a mental breakdown. He was unsuccessful, and declared bankruptcy. Later on, when he met his current wife, who was already spiritually awaken and who taught him to look at the world from another angle, Jan finally understood why he couldn't permanently succeed. Today, he owns a large company and makes a lot of money. He focused on wealth, stopped crying and blaming his problems on other people, and treats the issues he encounters as a call to take another step forward. He gives half of his profits to charity, without putting his name on the donation. He just gives.

Day One Hundred and Forty-Four of My New Era

If a person is ready, information from the spiritual path will flow freely. It sounds simple. This simplicity, however, has a natural enemy – our ego. This personal inner whisperer despises simplicity. Whenever an easy solution occurs, it immediately starts to complicate. Perhaps you are familiar with the sudden urge to find a more complicated solution, to improve on the banality, show that you can do more, that even a fool could figure out a simple solution, that you can do it better, more intelligently, enrich it with something and show everyone what you can do. My ego sometimes prevented me from accepting a simple thing. I experienced it when I, with some degree of success, used astrological forecasts to determine certain financial operations. I spent two years complicating everything and improved things until they became impossible, useless, until I lost myself in a sea of complications that made everything lose its sense. Things ceased to function and I couldn't go on. In school, they encouraged us to find simple solutions. At work, everyone raced to perfect, fulfill, expand, fueling egos that needed to be shown off, exhibited, emphasized, ignoring that it results in nothing. What matters is the affectation of public opinion, which fills us with a drug-like euphoria. Whoever wants to receive proof of their own greatness will receive proof of their own greatness, while those who want to live happy and meaningful lives will live happy and meaningful lives.

"*Wherever you go, there you are.*" -Thomas a Kempis

Day One Hundred and Forty-Five of My New Era

During a discussion on a web forum, I received a few questions. One of the askers wants to know how I can recognize a person who practices magic from a person on a genuine spiritual rise.

I do my best to see what this person does. If it's appropriate for all age groups, social groups, wealth, health, if it is a natural activity that enriches the person in all categories, then the person is on the rise. However, if their spiritual activities feature artificial props, unethical actions, parasitism, unnatural techniques, and hierarchies, then I know I am dealing with a manipulator.

Does the theory described in this book have a chance of succeeding in reality?

It can be easily applied in everyday life because it is simple, it cannot be argued with, it cannot be improved upon or filled in. Any change will make it dysfunctional. It is not burdened by the negative energy of history. It can only be proven in battle, not by pointless discussion. It is available to all without risk and it can bring into our lives everything we are ready for. This lifestyle is fair to everyone. If a person walking on this path fails, it is their own fault, and when they succeed, they will reach a point of reception. They will uncover new information and find out what was before concealed by darkness. They will perceive new vibrations and take a step forward in the evolutionary process. In my life, this method has succeeded.

Where are these pieces of spiritual information, where do they come from?

They are all around us. The problem is that we do not sense them. If we can tune to a matching, gentler frequency of their vibrations, we can access them. Only then can we correctly base our decisions on intuition and perhaps even communicate through telepathy and automatically perceive everything that is normally concealed.

How and from what are they made of?

Everything already exists; we do not create anything new. Everything is given and indestructible. If we feel that something new was made, it is only a feeling, when in reality it was a transformation of energy, arrangement into a different likeness.

Can I make any evolutionary progress if I agree with everything, but choose to be passive?

Being active is a necessity. Theories, books, studying, talking or parroting won't help. Lazy and passive people usually cannot formulate their own thoughts, relying instead on mimicking others. Only through our own work and effort can we look beneath the spiritual curtain. Only through regular care of our chakras, bodies, diets, positive outlooks, morality, ethics, connection with nature and distance from people and things that damage us can we make an evolutionary improvement

Why do some good, kind people suffer from heavy tragedies and failures throughout their lives while those who act immorally and unethically lead care-free and successful lives?

It is possible that during their past life, the person came very close to their evolutionary progress, and this life was supposed to serve as a way of straightening out small details and developing the self in areas of art or technology, a field they were previously unskilled in, so they could undergo balanced development without a build-up of karmic debts. Due to the lack of debts, this person succeeded and didn't experience any tragedies. Such person has either finished their quest, or they became a sluggard without progress, who abused their ideal standing and burdened their karma with negative energy that will come back to haunt them in the next life.

On the other side we have a hard-working, kind, virtuous, moral and selfless individual, who experiences never-ending bad luck, cannot succeed, is plagued by tragedies and illnesses one after another. No matter what they do, they live an unhappy life. It is possible they carried bad karmic build-up from past lives into this one, and the unbalanced layers are mercilessly exposed during the uncontrolled karmic cleansing. They encounter situations they hadn't handled during past lives, and need to act correctly this time around to clear them up.

During the course of one life we can cleanse ourselves of the mistakes made in past incarnations, but also those we made recently. The only way to avoid dramatic situations and serious illnesses is through care for the body, diet, chakras, positive feelings, and nature. Through this method, we achieve slow, systematic and gentle dissolution of karmic layers, a dissolution that will only be present through temporary physical discomfort.

How can we define the evolution of a person in the context of this book?

Encyclopedias usually explain evolution as an upward development. I'd like to define evolution as the level a person is tuned to.

Evolution of a person happens only inside the physical body and matter. A finely tuned human is able to easily and accurately distinguish between truth and lie, does not take part in killing of animals, does not eat meat, is moral, possesses high sense of ethics and a big dose of empathy, and resonates with similar energies. Such person does not judge with ego or reason because their feelings and will are balanced on the same level. They are calm, harmonious, and evenly developed.

I believe that the developmental step forward can be taken only when we harmonize ourselves and become a part of nature. For generations, we have known that we must protect the planet and nature so our children can survive, but we have done the opposite. This new path of sustainability, one I am proposing, begins with the human being. First, Homo sapiens must adopt a gentler approach, then apply changes that will save, sustain and regenerate the planet. People will act with absolute certainty. The path is simple and straightforward, as is everything valuable in life. The progress requires everyday exercise that leads to the opening of chakras, and presence in nature, where strong currents of bioenergy can pass through the open chakras and flow through a healthy and well-nourished body. Energies will bring us the information about everything we haven't been able to feel and perceive so far. We will be tuned to frequencies of the planet, nature, universe, and no one will think to damage the connection. It is a NEW way of sustainability.

Day One Hundred and Fifty of My New Era

One hundred and fifty days of a new lifestyle resulted in a great leap forward. I began to understand many things that were concealed from me in the past. For five months I daily exercised my chakras, and thanks to my natural diet I am able to keep them fully open, receive bioenergy from nature, keep my distance from harmful environments, things and people, and receive gentle vibrations and unexpected information. I am still at the beginning, and I still have many things to learn and improve on.

I realized that simplicity always holds a solution, that speaking and listening is really a way of life, that it's beneficial to replace the word 'problem' with the world 'opportunity', that one of the highest degrees of wisdom and communication is silence. A rose blossoms in silence and even this effort to rescue the humankind, our planet and nature will not be accompanied by trumpets or fireworks.

I wrote this book because I want to inspire others and share my own experience. It is a true story, not a book of fiction. I am not a doctor, scientists or nutritionist, but the information I gathered comes from established experts. Any reader who is interested in further research can find all of the information I've provided discussed in deeper detail online or in libraries. I haven't invented any of the theories in this book, only researched, collected, and tried them out on my own. They are logical, but only those who actually incorporate them into their daily routines can truly see what they are worth. Laying the foundations of a functional system took a lot of time, patience and work, but it has been the most wonderful adventure of my life so far, and it helped me finally understand how to properly live.

"*The person, who stares at me from the mirror changed significantly, stopped attacking me and I feel incredibly relieved.*" -Brona Fanelle

The End

References

Braden, G. (2008). The divine matrix: Bridging time, space, miracles, and belief. Carlsbad, CA: Hay House.

Brennan, B. (1988). Hands of light: A guide to healing through the human energy field. Ealing, England: Bantam Press.

Bohm, D. (2012). Quantum theory. New York: Dover Publication.

Budwig, J. (2012). Alternative cancer treatment. Retrieved from http://www.budwigcenter.com/anti-cancer-diet-php

Byrne, P. (2010). The many worlds of Hugh Everett III:Multiple universes, mutual assured destruction, and the meltdown of a nuclear family. New York, NY: Oxford University Press.

Clark, H. R. (2008). The cure and prevention of all cancers. Chula Vista, CA: New Century Press.

Diamond, H., Diamond, M. (1985). Fit for life. New York, NY: Grand Central Publishing.

Diamond, H., Diamond, M. (1987). Fit for life III: Living health the complete health program. New York, NY: Grand Central Publishing.

Emoto, M. (2005) The hidden messages in water. New York, NY: Atria Books.

Fife, B., Kabara, J. J. (2004). The coconut oil miracle. New York, NY: Penguin.

Griffin, E. (2010). World without cancer. Boca Raton, FL: American Media.

Kelmun, J. (n/d). Baking soda and maple syrup protocol. Retrieved from http://cancertutor.com/Cancer02/Kelmun.html

Malachov, G. (2008). Ocista tela a spravna vyziva- unikatni metodika uzdraveni. Prague, Czech Republic: Eugenika.

Mercola, J. (1997). Harvard study confirms fluoride reduces children's IQ. Retrieved form http://articles.mercola.com/sites/articles/archive/2012/08/14/fluoride-effects-in-children.aspx

Morse, R. (2004). The detox miracle source book. Chino Valley, CA: Hohm Press.

Redfield, J. (1997). The Celestine prophecy. New York, NY: Warner Books.

Walker, N. W. (1949). Become younger. Summertime, TN: Norwalk Press.

Walker, N. W. (1981). Natural weight control. Summertime, TN: Norwalk Press.

Walker, N. W. (1979). Colon health: The key to vibrant life. Summertime, TN: Norwalk Press.

Walker, N. W. (1970). Fresh vegetable and fruit juices. Summertime, TN: Norwalk Press.

Walker, N. W. (1974). Water can undermine your health. Summertime, TN: Norwalk Press.

Walker, N. W. (1972). The natural way to vibrant health. Summertime, TN: Norwalk Press.

Walker, N. W. (1971). The vegetarian guide to diet and salad. Summertime, TN: Norwalk Press.

Warburg, O. (1981). Otto Warburg: Cell physiologist, biochemist, and eccentric. New York, NY: Oxford University Press.

www.ingramcontent.com/pod-product-compliance
Lightning Source LLC
LaVergne TN
LVHW010915110826
845149LV00013B/2375

* 9 7 8 0 9 8 8 3 6 2 4 1 3 *